STEVE & SALLY BREEDLOVE
RALPH & JENNIFER ENNIS

the shame exchange

Trading Shame for God's Mercy and Freedom

NAVPRESS

NAVPRESS⟡

NavPress is the publishing ministry of The Navigators, an international Christian organization and leader in personal spiritual development. NavPress is committed to helping people grow spiritually and enjoy lives of meaning and hope through personal and group resources that are biblically rooted, culturally relevant, and highly practical.

**For a free catalog go to www.NavPress.com
or call 1.800.366.7788 in the United States or 1.800.839.4769 in Canada.**

ISBN: 978-1-60006-625-2

Cover design by The DesignWorks Group, Charles Brock
Cover image by Shutterstock

Some of the anecdotal illustrations in this book are true to life and are included with the permission of the persons involved. All other illustrations are composites of real situations, and any resemblance to people living or dead is coincidental.

Unless otherwise identified, all Scripture quotations in this publication are taken from the *Holy Bible, New International Version*® (NIV®). Copyright © 1973, 1978, 1984 by International Bible Society. Used by permission of Zondervan. All rights reserved. Other versions used include: the New American Standard Bible® (NASB), Copyright © 1960, 1962, 1963, 1968, 1971, 1972, 1973, 1975, 1977, 1995 by The Lockman Foundation. Used by permission; and *THE MESSAGE* (MSG). Copyright © 1993, 1994, 1995, 1996, 2000, 2001, 2002. Used by permission of NavPress Publishing Group.

Library of Congress Cataloging-in-Publication Data

Breedlove, Steve.
  The shame exchange : trading shame for God's mercy and freedom / Steve and Sally Breedlove, Ralph and Jennifer Ennis.
       p. cm.
  Includes bibliographical references (p.   ) and index.
  ISBN 978-1-60006-625-2 (alk. paper)
  1. Shame--Religious aspects--Christianity. I. Breedlove, Sally, 1950-
II. Title.
  BT714.B74 2009
  248.44--dc22

                                        2008047017

Printed in the United States of America

1 2 3 4 5 6 7 8 / 13 12 11 10 09

We may trust God with our past as heartily as with our future. It will not hurt us so long as we do not try to hide things, so long as we are ready to bow our heads in hearty shame where it is fit that we should be ashamed. For to be ashamed is a holy and blessed thing.

Shame is a thing to shame only those who want to appear, not those who want to be. Shame is to shame those who want to pass their examination, not those who want to get into the heart of things. . . . To be humbly ashamed is to be plunged into the cleansing bath of truth.

— *An Anthology of George McDonald,*

EDITED BY C. S. LEWIS

Contents

SAM'S STORY   7

INTRODUCTION: A CONVERSATION BEGINS   9

1. FEELING THE SHAME   17

2. POISONED BARBS AND DEEP WOUNDS   35

PAUSE TO LISTEN: LYDIA'S STORY   59

3. TRUE ROOTS AND FAULTY TACTICS   63

4. FACING MORE FAULTY TACTICS   87

PAUSE TO LISTEN: JACK'S STORY   111

5. THE VALLEY OF TROUBLE OR THE DOOR OF HOPE?   115

PAUSE TO LISTEN: RON'S STORY   129

6. A JOURNEY OVER TIME   133

7. BEAUTY FOR ASHES: THE SHAME EXCHANGE   143

8. A PLACE FOR ME AT THE TABLE   161

NOTES   187

ABOUT THE AUTHORS   189

Sam's Story

More times than can be counted, Sam has asked for forgiveness. But the pain of remembering outlasts every confession. That October evening when he was nineteen has marked his heart forever. Yes, he was going a little over the speed limit, but he wasn't drunk. He wasn't trying to kill, but his sister paid the price for his overreaction to a deer that ran across the country highway in front of his car. The deer lived. He lived. His sister died.

Sam's family and his friends told him how sorry they felt. That it wasn't his fault. That accidents happen. That they still loved him. Yet he knew he was going five miles over the speed limit. Everyone does five miles over the limit, but not everyone accidentally kills his sister doing it. If only.

Years have passed, but the event has never lost its power. Those around him have gone on with their lives. But he can't shake the barefaced reality that he killed his sister. No one else has ever called him a killer, but he is one to himself. It's a fact of life — this is his identity, embedded deep in his soul.

He doesn't deserve to be loved by anyone — not his parents, not his friends, not his wife, not his other sister, and certainly not God. Condemnation is what he needs — not the sappy Christian love he has heard about — because it fits the reality of what he has done.

The shame he feels has blocked his relationship with his wife and children. For years Kate has complained that he is a walled-in man, shutting out her and her love for him. Another failure. Now he senses that her love is growing tired. But all he feels is impotence, a deep sense that whatever he does, he is a flawed man.

A Conversation Begins

This is a book about shame. Your shame may not be like Sam's—nothing that tragic may have happened to you. But still, in your most honest moments, you know you have done things or had thoughts and feelings that are better left unexposed.

No one would blame you if you rejected this invitation to think about your shame. By definition, shame makes you feel really bad. It's far more than embarrassment—it's a profound sense of condemnation about who you are. It's a desire to hide because there are things you don't want anyone to know. It's a soul wretchedness that no amount of truth seems able to penetrate. It goes deeper than your actions and the guilt they may produce—it is about your identity, the fundamental perception of who you are.

When shame attacks, you try everything you can to get rid of it. You try to ignore it, pretending you have no shame, or drowning it out with a full calendar and a pair of earbuds, with drugs or alcohol. Maybe you simply distance yourself from the people who have heaped shame on you.

When that doesn't work, you try to fight your shame by labeling and analyzing it. You tell yourself all you need is some good self-talk—"If I can admit how angry that person makes me and convince myself how wrong he was, I'll feel better." But all too often that give-yourself-a-good-talking-to approach doesn't help. Sure, you had a brother who was cruel to you, but that's not the half of it. If anybody really knew what was going on inside your twisted mind, you'd be, well . . . ashamed.

Another tactic is escape through compensation. Shame's voice is nagging and persistent, but maybe achievement and success will drown it out. Or since you can't control what's happening inside of you, you find someone or something else to manipulate.

If you're a follower of Christ, you might turn to God and ask Him to simply take it away. You assume He sees shame as a bad thing. After all, He loves you and gave His only Son for you. It cost God a lot to make you part of His family, so He probably thinks it is not right for one of His children to feel shame. In fact, there must be something wrong with you if, as a follower of Christ, you feel ashamed. So you pray even harder that God will take away your shame.

But often that doesn't work, either. Why? Part of the problem is that we think God deals with shame the same way He deals with guilt. But shame and guilt are different. Guilt at its core is about specific actions that violate standards we are supposed to live up to. True guilt can be a good thing. As we become aware of the wrong things we have done, as we realize we're guilty of breaking God's laws, we recognize our need for a Savior who will forgive us.

Even after we are on the path of following Christ, guilt can continue to help us. It alerts us to the things in our lives that are a far cry from the character of Christ. If we want Christ's friendship, if we want His pleasure with our lives, we learn to admit what we have done (confession) and to ask His forgiveness.

Recently I (Sally) said something caustic about a friend. As I did, I realized he was in earshot. Whether or not he overheard, I was wrong to say what I did. Until I went to that person, owned what I did, and asked for forgiveness, I could not be at peace with him. Fortunately this man forgave me. On the other side of that hard conversation, I felt relief from my guilt and gladness that the relationship had been restored.

It works the same way with God. He promises in the Scriptures that if we admit what we've done that is contrary to His will, He will forgive us. When we talk honestly with God, we have the opportunity to experience forgiveness and a restored relationship.

As crazy as it seems, guilt can be a gift. Shame is different. It's rarely about some act we did that was wrong—it's about who we are. No amount of confession or self-lecturing on God's forgiveness will remove our sense of shame. We become more convinced than ever that something is profoundly wrong with us.

Does God have a better answer? Surprisingly, a closer look at the Scriptures reveals that God doesn't necessarily take our approach of understanding the problem and moving toward an immediate and quick solution. In fact, God's Word says things about our shame that we may not like or understand. But He says them anyway.

For example, in a time when his nation lay languishing from its sin, the prophet Jeremiah spoke harsh words to the stubborn-hearted Jews: "Therefore the showers have been withheld, and no spring rains have fallen. Yet you have the brazen look of a prostitute; *you refuse to blush with shame*" (3:3, emphasis added). Rather than trying to make the nation feel better, Jeremiah wanted them to experience their shame.

Ezekiel, another prophet during that same time period, had been deported to Babylon during the great resettlement of the Jewish people by their captors. Along with the rest of the Jews, he suffered the discipline of God. His message was not just about forgiveness or a future hope; he also called the Israelites to something anyone would want to avoid.

This is what the Sovereign LORD says: It is not for your sake, O house of Israel, that I am going to do these

things, but for the sake of my holy name, which you
have profaned among the nations where you have gone.
I want you to know that I am not doing this for your
sake . . . *Be ashamed and disgraced for your conduct, O
house of Israel!* (36:22,32, emphasis added)

A number of years later God gave the prophet Daniel a
panoramic picture of God's work throughout the civilizations
of men. With that vision God also called him to act as His
spokesman and as a mentor to the kings of the Persian Empire.
Daniel's response to such a high position may be surprising. It's
not just gratitude he felt or a desire to carry out God's calling
with faithfulness. In his response to God he brought up the
issue of shame: "Lord, you are righteous, but this day *we are
covered with shame* . . . O LORD, we and our kings, our princes
and our fathers are *covered with shame* because we have sinned
against you" (9:7-8, emphasis added).

Shame shows up in the New Testament as well. In one of
the most uncomfortable conversations in the Bible, Jesus used
shame as He talked with the Canaanite woman in Matthew
15:21-28. She asked for deliverance for her demon-possessed
daughter, but Jesus rejected her request because she was not a
Jew. She persisted in asking, and He responded, "It is not good
to take the children's bread and throw it to the dogs" (verse 26,
NASB). (Imagine saying something like that when your neigh-
bor asks for prayer for her daughter!) Interestingly the woman
didn't reject His harsh words about her shamefulness; instead
she received them.

If Jesus is as loving as the Bible says He is, why would He want to make a person feel ashamed? His willingness to expose our shame is hardly encouraging if we think the only appropriate response to shame is to get rid of it as quickly as possible.

But as we listen to these passages from both the Old and New Testaments, we see God reminding us of our shame. *Learning what it means to face, and in some sense embrace, our shame is a major theme of this book.* But don't stop reading yet.

Facing our shame is the door to profound healing. But if that is so, how do we do it? To begin, we need to slow down and let the voice of shame deep within our souls speak to us. We need to be touched by the pervasive shame that fills our culture and understand that it won't easily go away. We need to explore all the strategies we have invented to keep our shame at bay. We need to see Jesus, the one who Himself took on shame, bearing it in His own body and absorbing its power.

The walk toward shame is really a walk toward the love of God. As we make that walk together in this book, we will come to see the beauty that emerges as we face our shame while clinging to the hand of the God of all mercy.

The four people writing this book are two married couples who share a friendship. We met in an Italian restaurant ten years ago, introduced by mutual friends who hoped we would connect. We did, and since then we have talked. A lot. About ideas and the culture we live in, about the sheer joy and deep pain of raising a family (we have nine children, seven children-in-law, and fourteen grandchildren between us). About the everyday realities of work and about having too little time.

About the heartaches and questions that persist in the midst of all that is good. But more than anything we have wrestled through our beliefs and understandings about God, life, community, and service within His kingdom. At times we have taken the Scriptures and held them up like a prism, praying God would give us light so that the beauty of what He says would fall in its manifold color upon us.

Early in our friendship, Ralph became intrigued by the pervasive sense of shame that he saw emerging in American culture. This seemed like a sea change. All four of us had grown up in a world where we learned to deny shame, run from it, or expect the gospel to quickly fix it. Why were movies, art, music, and literature now speaking directly about shame?

Ralph suggested that we explore this forbidden territory. We agreed, wanting to understand it for ourselves and hoping to be able to live more authentically because of it. Perhaps we would discover better, truer ways of dealing with shame. Perhaps we would learn something that would help someone else.

When we all agreed to the project, we read books, studied Scripture, and conducted interviews. At first, it was an interesting, theoretical discussion. It was also safe. But then we hit a wall. If we were writing an authentic book about shame, we had to acknowledge our own shame. Like most people, we were reluctant to do this.

But if we could not step out of self-protection into mutual self-disclosure, then all the things we were learning about the benefits and healing that come as we face our shame would only be theory. In fact, if we were unwilling to talk, we would be agreeing with the internal voices that tell us not to risk exposure. So we made a plan. We would tell our stories. We would speak about ourselves and about our pasts in the way that only our spouses or our counselors or our closest friends had ever heard. (Remember, as we began this conversation, we had been friends for only a year or so.) We knew instinctively that if we hoped to experience true friendship, we had to talk. And we knew from our study of Scripture that God could bring great good from our shame. To share openly was to walk by faith into these truths. So we planned a time and a place. We even drew straws for who would go first, second, third, fourth. And then we talked. What we said to each other is blended in this book with the stories other people have so graciously shared with us. You should also know that, unless noted otherwise, the first-person voice in this book is Sally's.

Our prayer for you is the same prayer we have for ourselves. We pray that as you enter into the dialogue of this book, you will acknowledge your own shame. In that acknowledgment, may the words spoken within this book and, more than that, the words God speaks in His Holy Scriptures themselves, take you on a journey deep into the merciful heart of God.

CHAPTER ONE

Feeling the Shame

When we started this project, I (Sally) wasn't so sure that I had an issue with shame. I am a firstborn with a built-in drive toward perfectionism. Guilt I get. It's what I feel every time I don't measure up to my own standards, much less God's. But shame . . . well, that's for people who fail a lot, who just don't have the chutzpah to achieve. I have always been determined not to be one of them.

But as I listened to the stories of everyone we interviewed and as I talked with my husband Steve and with Ralph and Jennifer, my carefully buried shame began to emerge. It lay hidden beneath my drive to achieve and to project an image of worthiness. I realized I needed healing too.

You may find the same thing happening in your heart as you read this book. We encourage you to enter the difficult process of facing and experiencing your shame. It is natural to resist. Shame does not want to be exposed. It's elusive, quick to rename itself. It takes on many disguises, vociferously blaming others. The stories in this chapter may help you. They are true stories of men and women of different ages and ethnicities. We have changed names and details to protect confidentiality, but the circumstances and feelings are accurately and fairly described.

You may be one of those people who says, "Skip the story part; just tell me what I need to know." But we learn by listening to the lives of others, and we encourage you to take the time to read the stories in this chapter and throughout the book. As you read, you may wish you could help these people see they don't have to feel ashamed. The insensitivity, selfishness, and wickedness of others were wrong and not their fault. You may get angry at those who did the wounding. You may want to remind the storytellers that God doesn't see them the way they see themselves.

Resist these urges. Instead let these stories help you ask important questions: Where does shame come from? Is it always from something outside of me? Or is there some shame I bear that cannot be explained away as "something someone else did to me"? We will have time enough as we make our way through this book to differentiate between the shame that others put on us and the true shame that we really need to own.

And don't worry! We won't leave you there. It is only the first step on the path to a brighter, freer life.

FRANCES

Jennifer and I traveled to meet Frances, an African American woman, at a crisis pregnancy center in a nearby city where she serves as director. It was a cold December afternoon, but as we entered her office, the sun streaming through the window warmed the room. Rising from her chair, Frances welcomed us and then shut the door so that we could talk openly. As her story unfolded, the tranquility of that winter afternoon contrasted sharply with the childhood she had endured.

"I've always known shame," she said, "not by name but by the dark, suffocating weight I've carried inside me from my earliest memories. When you're poor and black, the world puts shame on you—it's a given in our culture."

Mixed into that racial shame was a stinging embarrassment about her body. She had always hated how fat she was. The kids at school called her "the blimp." Her parents did not teach her even the basics of personal hygiene. The taunts of other children made her realize that they saw her not only as fat but also as dirty and ugly.

If that wasn't enough, her teeth were crooked, protruding, and unevenly spaced. But her parents mocked her the few times she gathered up the courage to ask if they could be fixed. Teeth, weight, race, and hygiene—it all added up to a potent brew of shame.

Frances reached into her purse, found her wallet, and pulled out an old picture from its hiding place behind a credit card. The little girl who stared at us had that blown-up look of true obesity. Her pigtails were tied with twine; her dress was a dismal hand-me-down; her tight-lipped smile hid her teeth but also contorted her face.

As we looked at her photograph, Frances recounted the memories that picture held for her of the fourth grade. All the other girls had come to school scrubbed, in their best dresses, with ribbons in their hair, ready for the annual picture day. But her parents and her teacher had let her sit in front of the camera in an ugly, worn-out dress with her hair a mess. That day was her first encounter with shame's power to stab the heart.

Frances's family lived in the projects; her father had a secure government job; and they went to church. Those things should have represented a measure of goodness, but it was only a façade. Behind the surface, shame had a special place in Frances's home—its power multiplied by the darkness in her family.

The afternoon light was fading as she talked. Frances turned on a lamp beside her desk, and her words came more slowly. Her father's drunkenness and rage fueled the sexual and physical abuse he forced upon his three children. The pain of what he did to them made the issues of poverty, ugliness, and race pale in significance. The children had nowhere to turn for protection. The African American culture itself locked them in. Family honor was key. To ask for help, to look for comfort or safety outside the family, was a greater wrong than what was happening to them.

As she moved into her teen years, the world beyond her family compounded her shame. Frances attended a middle-class school, bused there by government mandate. But no teacher or guidance counselor encouraged her or helped her see her potential. The school simply endured her presence. Whatever life she might have dared to dream about was choked almost to death by the loneliness and cynicism she encountered at every turn.

As she neared adulthood, sexual experimentation, alcohol, drugs, and listlessness occupied her days. But even in the good moments she attempted to wring from sex or alcohol, she still felt trapped, suffocating under a blanket of shame. *If you're trash, you might as well do trashy things*, she would say to herself. So she did. Again and again. Better to believe she was garbage and act on it than risk hoping at all for something better.

Then, in her early twenties, Frances met a group of Christians who accepted her and helped her believe she wasn't doomed. She decided she had had enough. She wanted to make something of her life. She finished her GED so she would have a high-school diploma, and then she won a full scholarship to a good university. Frances made a vow during that time: She would be strong enough to protect herself and strong enough to find ways to fit in as a successful person. But success did not take away the horrible voice inside whispering that the real Frances was too dreadful for others to see.

Years passed. The Christian friends she had made kept loving her. She learned to open up and trust them, to let them know her secrets. She found a good counselor; she gave up the destructive habits that had plagued her life. Frances is now in her early forties. As we sat with her in her office, we sensed her peace. The warmth in the room came not just from the afternoon sunlight as it streamed through the window but also from her.

Can shame like Frances has endured really be that profoundly healed? Can a person find freedom from shame's power? The questions begged for an answer.

Seeing the profound freedom in Frances was one of the best moments in our interview process. Her shame was obvious and understandable, but surprisingly she seemed to be moving toward substantial restoration in her life. Her story confirmed what we were learning in our own lives—it really is possible to exchange our shame for the mercy and love of God. How we make that exchange is, of course, the topic of this whole book.

No matter what has happened to you, God stands ready to begin the work in your own life of trading in your shame for His mercy and love.

CLAIRE

Jennifer and I talked to Claire a number of times, and her story emerged slowly. As we began, I wondered if Claire really had any shame. Her life seemed immune to the possibility. Her family represented Old Southern stock, vestiges of landed gentry or American nobility, a background few can claim. For generations Claire's family had been at the center of its city's culture and power. Her great-grandparents bought property in what became one of the most prestigious parts of the city and then passed that land down to the next two generations, subdividing it as it became more valuable. A view of the river filled her family's living-room window, and a deep sense of heritage filled her heart.

Claire's family had heroes. A few were well-known American leaders and philanthropists. Others had made significant contributions in the worlds of finance and education. Oil paintings of these heroes were distributed between the houses of her large extended family; everyone had a famous relative looking over his or her shoulder. To that gallery Claire has added other people she admired. She is a relentless reader, and biographies are her favorite.

She took it all in, she told us, absorbing the motto her family lived by: *To whom much is given, from them will much be expected.* To be somebody, you had to do something. Early in life, she determined to live up to this standard.

In many ways, she succeeded. Scrapbooks and photo albums tell the story of the honors she won during her high-school and university years. "Most people would have described me as a wonderful young woman," Claire said, her voice tense over the phone, "but all I felt was a drivenness to achieve more. In my mind, I was mediocre. Who would ever write my biography? My name would never be a Wikipedia entry, much less in a history book. I'd probably never even have my own oil portrait hanging in a grandkid's dining room."

Once Claire married, her moderate level of success haunted

her. If she were really good, really worthwhile, she would have accomplished something important by now. She began to doubt her intelligence, her self-discipline, her abilities, even her husband's love.

Then came motherhood. Parenting was harder than she thought it would be. Her children did not respond to her as she expected. She had been close to her mother and her grandmothers—admiring them, wanting to be like them. Why didn't her children feel the same way toward her? Had she overidealized her own childhood? Did she have difficult kids? Was she flawed as a mother? She had been given so much—didn't that mean God expected a lot from her?

As Jennifer and I talked with her over several months, Claire admitted to things she never felt she could say out loud, to anyone. "I hate what a depressing, complaining woman I'm becoming," she said. "Am I really the only person in my family struggling with worthlessness? I know that everyone else thinks I am so close to having it all. I tell myself I ought to be content and at peace, but I'm not."

Self-talk doesn't help. Neither does her faith. She leads a Bible study at her church, but by the next morning, the ache is back. Her friendships bring little relief. She'll have lunch with a group of women she really likes, the conversation will go well, but when it is over, she feels that she didn't measure up. Why can't she gratefully embrace what she's been given and believe life is good?

Claire continues to hash it out with the two of us. She has heard our stories as well. Maybe her struggles lie in her temperament (was she born morose or fearful?), or perhaps she isn't grateful enough. Maybe she tries too hard or not hard enough. Fundamentally she just feels bad about feeling bad. How can shame be a problem when most people would say she hasn't failed at all, that she has been so extravagantly loved?

What do you think? Is Claire's problem a shame problem? Or is she just too introspective? If that is true, what makes a person so introspective?

CORNELIUS

Cornelius took time off from packing his house to talk to me (Steve). Everything but a few clothes and books were going into storage for at least a year. Within a few weeks Cornelius and his family would be somewhere in California. After four months there, maybe to Malaysia, then perhaps on around the world to Europe—but they weren't sure. It was to be a year without pressure, so what was the point of planning so far ahead?

Though we were just sitting down to coffee, Cornelius launched into the interview with amazing candor. "My family traces their Christian heritage back to missionary work in China in the nineteenth century. Hudson Taylor himself told the story of salvation to my great-great-grandfather. Each generation since has passed on the truth of Christ; it's from my own family that I learned the gospel. But it's also from them that I inherited the chains of cultural rules and expectations, a prison my family brought with them when they immigrated to America."

For four generations, it was clear that the oldest son in the family was dedicated to Christian work; the others were dedicated to professional accomplishments. Cornelius was the second son, expected to be the intellectual and professional star.

But even in elementary school, he struggled. He was a decent student, but the hard work it took to maintain a B average made it clear that he would never be accepted at a prestigious university. His cousins had chosen Stanford, Harvard, MIT, and the University of Chicago. The eldest sons among his cousins dutifully took up the mantle of Christian work. The rest chose advanced degrees that led to respected careers.

Everyone around him was living up to the family code, but try as he would, Cornelius simply could not make the grade. He dreaded high-school graduation, knowing he would fail the family system.

But something else in the mix made it even harder on his parents.

Cornelius sipped his coffee and looked out the window. "I love sports and military history," he said. "What I really wanted to do was go to West Point. But my parents couldn't stand the idea. They had left Hong Kong as they saw the gathering storm of World War II. Few things are more shameful to them than a military career. They forbade me to join the high-school ROTC, but I did it anyway."

One of the lowest days of his life, a day that twenty-seven years later still feels like a kick in his stomach, occurred in early September of his tenth-grade year. His parents surprised him by showing up at school during his drill practice. In full view of all his buddies, they yelled at Cornelius and the commanding officer. Cornelius dropped the class, but deep inside he vowed he would never give up again. He would stick to his guns and take more risks despite the heavy weight of his family's disapproval.

This vow began to work its way into the fabric of his decision-making. As he pursued his relationship with God at university, Cornelius concluded that he was called to Christian ministry as a pastor. Yes, it was against the established family rules, but his older brother, the one who had been given the generational mantle of ministry, wanted nothing to do with God. It seemed logical to Cornelius that his parents should applaud his ambition. But again he was disappointed. In their minds circumstances should not alter what was meant to be. Cornelius was meant to get an education and find a lucrative profession. That was his place in the family.

Cornelius's frustration and anger clouded his sense of joy and purpose as he trained for ministry. The nagging pull of shame was always with him—he had let his parents down. If only he had been smarter, if only he had been more of the son they expected.

As he entered full-time ministry, his parents' shame at his choices receded into the background. Other things stirred up his sense of impotency. Leading a Chinese American church was more difficult than he had imagined. He preached as sincerely and as well as he knew how. He tried to care for people, to be a spiritual man, to lead his congregation, but nothing really happened. The church barely grew.

The congregation reminded him of his own family. Most of the parents in his church had only two goals for their children: academic success and financial prosperity. Music lessons were the only acceptable after-school activity. Most families were inconsistent in their church attendance. If it wasn't exam season, they were traveling the state for music competitions. As a pastor, he could not crack the code of values and expectations his people embraced. He was failing to break the larger cultural system, just as he had failed to break it in his own family.

New questions troubled his soul, questions that carried their own reproach. Maybe he had missed God's will in refusing to submit to his parents' wishes. Maybe his mediocrity was not just academic but also spiritual.

"I know the 'right' answers here," Cornelius said. "I know that true spiritual success in God's eyes cannot be measured by numbers—it only comes from being loved by God and from living a faithful life." He shrugged his shoulders. "In my mind, I've still failed, and I've had enough."

Choosing the pastorate against his parents' wishes had been a real risk, but it still left so many unanswered questions inside. Perhaps his choice had not been radical enough. Now at age forty, he was determined to do exactly what he wanted to do. It was crazy, but he wanted to do something to break the hold other people's expectations had on him. He was tired of his sense of public shame and the personal inadequacy controlling his decisions. His wife was a successful investment adviser and had made enough money to take an extended time off. His three children were just entering their teens, and if he diddn't act now, they would never be able to do this as a family.

I had been at the coffee shop for almost two hours listening to Cornelius's story. As he finished, we sat without speaking, watching through the plateglass window as the sun disappeared from the horizon.

Cornelius hesitated, then spoke once more. "I'm glad we are leaving. I'm looking forward to a whole year without a BlackBerry or cell phone or daily e-mail checks. I'm looking forward to being with Ruth and the girls. But you know what? I really don't think it's going to stop the voices inside. How do you ever get away from the sense that you will never live up to anybody's dreams, not even your own?"

Cornelius's story leaves us with a troubling question: Even if you break the system, can you silence the voice of shame?

WHAT WE'VE DISCOVERED FROM THE STORIES

As you have read the stories of Frances, Claire, and Cornelius, you may have noticed that your story has some of the same elements. That certainly happened to us.

Again and again we concluded that we all have uneasy voices muttering in our hearts. No one is exempt from the power of shame. Everyone struggles on some level with the troubling thought that all is not well with my soul.

It's easy to see the work of shame in Frances's life. Harsh things happened to her—sexual abuse, her father's alcoholic rages, the shame of being dark skinned in a white-dominated culture, the choices she made.

Her story contains another common, compounding element of shame: No matter what was done to her, if she broke the code of silence and looked for help, she would have exposed her family and brought an even greater shame on them all. The people around her would have judged her more harshly than they judged her father. She would have been cast out. In Frances's world the ultimate "wrong" is to dishonor one's family or community. She inhabits what is called a "shame/honor" culture. Such a world works to keep bad behaviors in check, but it can also hide other, more destructive behaviors. And it certainly offers no healing balm for damaged hearts.

The real problem is that shame won't stay locked up inside. Trying to contain shame is like putting hydrochloric acid in a tin can. The acid can't be contained forever. It will spill out on others and do its corroding work in the lives of those closest to us. And it will eat at us, just as acid eats at a tin can, so that we are destroyed. No heart is impervious. By the time she was eight, Frances knew the corroding power of shame, but she was helpless in the face of it.

Some people might protest that no one can grow up in a

society like Frances's and *not* feel the weight of shame. Some Christians argue that a truer worldview sees life from the perspective of a guilt/law orientation.

The guilt/law worldview goes something like this: If a person violates a standard God has set, then he or she is guilty and should feel guilty. The solution is some form of punishment and/or restitution. The good news of Christianity is that Christ's death on the cross means Christ took on the punishment for our sins. Since the punishment has been exacted, we are no longer guilty and should not feel guilty anymore. Our responsibility is to ask God's forgiveness and trust Christ's death on the cross as the payment for our sins. From a guilt/law perspective, a struggle with shame means you just haven't confessed everything you've done wrong or you haven't exercised faith to receive the forgiveness God has offered.

The trouble is, for many Christians, the shame still won't go away. They have believed as well as they know how. They have confessed, surrendered, rededicated, prayed, and believed again. But shame still whispers to them.

Think about Claire. Her family knew success and public approval. She has never done anything "really bad," and nothing "really bad" has ever happened to her. Yet she cannot overcome the troubling thought that something is wrong with her. Shame is embedded deep, and it seems to have few explanations.

Many of us, regardless of the roots of our shame, adopt a common strategy to handle it. We make vows, promising ourselves we will never do something again, that we will never let a certain thing happen to us again. We promise ourselves that we will accomplish a certain goal, take up a certain course of action. In these vows we look for protection—not just from the world, but from the pain inside our souls.

Cornelius made several vows, each one an attempt to establish himself, to feel right about who he was. Claire made a vow even though she did not realize it. As a young girl looking at all her well-known relatives enshrined in portraits, she promised the generations before her that one day she would be famous and justify her existence before God and before them.

Vow-making is a strategy with some short-term positive effects. It takes a person's mind off the pain. It offers self-protection and a course of action when he or she doesn't want to hurt anymore or be the victim waiting for the next blow.

The end result of vows, however, is that they often hurt more than help. They freeze your vision (*does Claire really need to be famous to be significant?*). They hurt your heart (*is determining to break free from all expectations helpful or hurtful to Cornelius?*). They keep us hidden (*by not revealing her father's abuse, did Frances find healing or did it make her more isolated?*). Vows can appear to help us, and often, for a while, they do. But in the end, we need a better cure for our shame than vows.

We will listen to other stories along the way, but now we need to shift our focus from other people so that we can take a look at our own lives.

Pause to Reflect

Perhaps you have never recognized the voice of shame within your own heart. Start with these simple questions:

When do you feel embarrassed? Do you know why those things embarrass you?

What do you hope no one will ever discover about you?

Take a look at the following words and listen to how your heart responds to them:

- Failure
- Inadequate
- Powerless
- Condemned

If one of these words carries "emotional weight" for you, journal about it or talk it out with a friend you trust.

What are you afraid of? Why?

Are you aware of vows you have made that you hope will protect you or give you a sense that you are okay?

Think back through the stories in this chapter. Who did you identify with? What have you done to avoid or conquer your own sense of shame?

If you are able, briefly journal your story of shame.

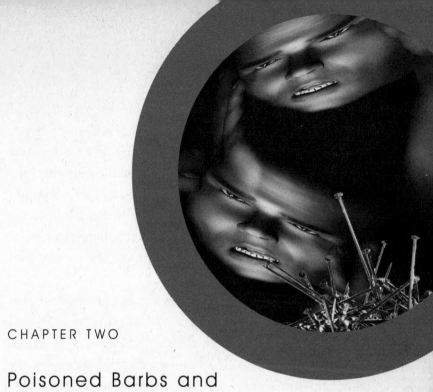

CHAPTER TWO

Poisoned Barbs and Deep Wounds

> Woe to him who gives drink to his neighbors,
>> pouring it from the wineskin till they are drunk,
>> so that he can gaze on their naked bodies.
> You will be filled with shame instead of glory.
>> Now it is your turn! Drink and be exposed!
> The cup from the LORD's right hand is coming around
>> to you,
>> and disgrace will cover your glory.
>> (Habakkuk 2:15-16)

The indigenous people of the Amazon rainforest have perfected the use of poisonous barbed arrows for hunting and warfare. The harlequin skin of certain beautifully colored frogs contains toxins that can kill a tapir—or a man—within moments. The natives have learned to distill the poison and create a potion into which they dip their arrowheads. Barbs quickly force the arrowheads deep into the skin, ensuring that the poison enters the bloodstream. No antidotes exist for most of these powerful poisons.

The stories we shared in the previous chapter illustrate that shame works in a similar fashion. Words, attitudes, actions, and events are barbed arrowheads that penetrate our souls and poison us with shame. Over the years, the message that we are flawed proves resistant to almost every antidote, no matter how skillfully applied. Often, the more we try to resolve our shame or get rid of it, the more it embeds itself in our souls.

For example, I (Steve) became friends with a young man in a church where I pastored. I knew a lot about Dan because I knew his parents and he joined a study I taught. After a few months of hanging around to talk after the study, he asked if we could have coffee. We met within two days, but despite his earlier interest in getting together, it seemed like the conversation was going nowhere.

He hesitated and then asked, "Do you really want to know what I am thinking?"

I nodded "of course," and he began to unfold the story of his loneliness. As his feelings gained momentum, he exploded in a passionate expression of worthlessness. I didn't know what to say, but then my pastoral training kicked in. I began to recite all the truth I knew in an effort to fix his feelings.

It didn't work. All of my efforts to remind him of his accomplishments (many), his friends (more than most), his abilities (plainly visible), his physical prowess (a star athlete), and his spiritual well-being (a sincere follower of Jesus Christ) could not relieve the shame within.

My logical and true statements about reality only increased the fear gnawing at his heart. Reminding him of truth that did not touch his heart only exacerbated the problem. His conversation-ending words were, "You just don't understand. There's something wrong with me. I feel like crap. In fact, I *am* crap!"

Dan's story helped me realize that in searching for the sources of shame in a person's life, explanations often fail and self-understanding runs dry. Shame is just *there*. We can't always trace it back to a life-altering choice we made or some abuse that was dealt to us. Claire, whom you met in the last chapter, would agree. And Cornelius, who is aware that he has been wounded by his culture and his family, is not healed by that awareness. Understanding where our shame comes from does not banish the shame. Often the harder we work to overcome our shame, the deeper it seeps into our hearts. Our efforts are further proof that the problem is within, in who we are. We become increasingly convinced that we are flawed, that we will inevitably fail, that our lives will never amount to much.

How do these barbs of shame enter our souls in the first place? How do they pierce and poison us? In this chapter we'll describe some of the ways that shame finds its way into our hearts. As you read, you will probably find that your own heart has been affected by one or more of these barbs.

PERFORMANCE SHAME: THE BARB OF FAILURE

We sometimes do things we can't undo. We break things we cannot totally mend. We may ask for forgiveness, but it doesn't resolve the feelings. Adulteries committed, friends betrayed, greed habituated—these things reveal something dark inside and beg the question, "What kind of person would _____ (insert your shameful deed)? I thought I was better than this. What a _____ (insert disparaging noun) I am."

We began this book with a brief look into the heart of a man named Sam who believed he killed his sister in a freak car wreck. His lifelong burden of shame is robbing him of hope for healing. It is threatening his marriage. It is fed by the memory of an act—a single event Sam blames himself for in spite of the fact that everyone else accepts it as an accident.

Not all performance shame is rooted in visible or catastrophic actions. It is often subtle, hiding deep in the foliage of the heart. It can be birthed in the failure to meet your own standard of success. You do not get into the grad school you hoped for. You remember seasons of sitting on the bench in high-school football. In the midst of a piano recital, the music vaporizes out of your mind. When things like that happen, the voice accuses, "You didn't just fail; *you are a failure.*" The barb of performance shame latches on to everything it can to drive its accusation home.

Performance shame also penetrates the soul through the words and actions of other people. "We don't want that idiot in our study group" or "That klutz can't be on our team" can be communicated by a simple look, a repeated rejection. Do you recall those moments on the playground when the two captains chose their teams? If you were one consistently chosen last, you can probably still feel the burn of shame.

Our friends (Steve and Sally's) who raised their children in Europe still regret subjecting them to the routine shame that accompanied their schooling. The school system seated elementary children in the classroom according to their grade point average. They understood that their parents did not expect them to be seated in the "first chair." They understood that school was harder for them because their first language was English. But sitting in the last chair, in the back of the room, still spoke volumes: *You must be dumb. You are in last place, and everyone knows it.* Every failure (perceived or real) that we experience can twist that barb of performance shame into our souls.

I (Sally) recently gave a talk in front of a large group. Several sentences became so tangled up that I had trouble completing my thoughts. By the time I sat down, the barb of shame was doing its work. Later that day I told my husband how badly I had done. He said, "I thought you did a great job." Over the years I have found him to be an honest critic. His response gave me pause—why do I so easily focus on what I do poorly and fail to see what I do well?

Performance shame goes surprisingly deep. Most of us can identify with some area of performance that we, our families, or our culture deems essential. If you struck out a whole season of baseball, you probably weren't comforted by the words "It's just a game." Deep down you believe those strikeouts proved an undeniable fact of reality. Something is wrong with you, and your failure at bat is glaring evidence for the world to see.

IMAGE SHAME: THE BARB OF LOSING FACE

In some cultures, performance shame is not just the way people naturally (and sometimes wickedly) treat each other; it is actually an acceptable motivational tool. Those who have authority or power use it to shape behavior and produce results. When this happens, the shame that comes from poor performance is tied to image shame, losing face in the eyes of other people.

Shame/honor cultures that capitalize on image shame are common around the world. Traditionally the Western world has operated more from a guilt/law perspective. From that point of view, if you break the law, you should feel guilty. Guilt is a good thing. It helps you to know what you have done wrong so that you will hopefully make some sort of restitution. Furthermore, because guilt produces negative feelings, wanting to avoid it can keep us from wrong behavior.

But as we in the West become more ethnically diverse, other cultural perspectives are woven into the fabric of our society. In a shame/honor culture, poor behavior or performance not only shames you as an individual, but worse, it shames the group you represent. Your family, friends, or race are affected by what you do. As harsh as it may seem, this sort of shaming is not meant to destroy the inner character of the person but to motivate him to perform well and uphold the family or cultural reputation.

Regardless of the motivation, public shaming and losing face can be devastating. Few people retain a deep sense of personal worth when they are openly shamed. The arrow goes deep. One man raised in a shame-based culture told us that it was normal for his teachers to grab a paper off his desk and begin to ridicule his work in front of the class. He said the teachers typically conducted discipline in front of the class as well. The goal was to motivate the class to perform better and live up to the standards of family and group honor.

But for this man, the public shaming was deadly. He saw himself as a continual failure. He believed the teacher's reproach exposed a secret, unsolvable problem within his soul. And he wasn't just letting himself down—he was a blight on his family, his school, and his culture. He handled the shame by vowing never to admit that he was wrong or that he had failed. He would always "save face."

In his forties he was fired from his job. When the firing became publicly known, the exposure took him to the brink of suicide. Only an extended time of healing with a counselor helped him see that losing face was not the final statement about who he was.

Image shaming shows up in the critical undertones of parents' interaction with their children. Think of the snatches of conversation you have heard at the mall, at the grocery store, at your child's ballgame, from your childhood, or from your own mouth: *I don't like to take you shopping with me—you are such a bad boy. I can't get anything done with you here . . . You're embarrassing me . . . Look at the way your sister is sitting. Her manners are so good; yours are horrible. Next time we eat out, I want to leave you home . . . I can't believe you fumbled that ball; I never thought one of my sons would be so clumsy.*

One of our sons (Steve and Sally's) was at a skateboard park recently. He watched a father come up to a young child, grab her by the wrist, and say, "I can't believe you didn't get that trick right. You'd better next time, or we're leaving. You're embarrassing me." This little five-year-old girl was bearing the weight of her father's public image through her performance at a skate park! Words like those can remain embedded in the soul forever.

It goes on into adulthood. *I'd expect somebody who has been here as long as you have to know the answer to that question. I would think someone in your position in this company would have been able to solve that problem. Your sister's children certainly are better behaved than yours. Knowing your family, I'm surprised you didn't go to college. I'll bet your dad hoped you would become a doctor like he is. Most of our graduates have had a wide choice of job offers to choose from.*

Performance and image shame are similar but not identical. Performance shame is rooted in abilities and behavior, in self-image. Image shame deals primarily with the fears of how others see us. The two often work in tandem, feeding and reinforcing each other. You can fail to live up to an internal standard of performance, and that failure is multiplied by your sense that those around you will be disappointed and even ashamed by your failure. Knowing you have failed them as well as yourself compounds your sense of worthlessness. Together, these twin barbs tell you that you are a failure to be held up for the world to see and ridicule. If you believe this message, performance and image shame will spread their poison in your soul.

VICTIM SHAME: THE BARB OF ABUSE

Victim shame is spawned when a person is violated sexually, physically, economically, or emotionally. Victims often bear more shame than their abusers do—at first blush, it doesn't seem to make sense, but it is true. A five-year-old is never to blame when she is sexually abused by her thirty-five-year-old uncle, but more often than not she will struggle with great personal shame. Her self-reproach is rooted in a belief that the abuse was somehow her fault.

When the wounds of the victim are left unhealed, he or she often chooses destructive sexual relationships or destructive behaviors as a teenager or adult. At that point, the abused can become a willing participant or even a perpetrator in the cycle of abuse. If he believes he is just as bad as, or maybe even worse than, the one who abused him, then he is more likely to abuse down the line just as he was also abused.

What happens when our sexual response is aroused prematurely or inappropriately? Even when it happens in the earliest years of childhood, consequences still roll out from that violation. For example, a young teenage girl may experience confusing, disturbing sexual responses to older men or an equally disturbing inability to relate to the good young men who are interested in getting to know her better. She may not know exactly why she feels the way she does, but something inside says that there is something wrong with her and that she is not worthy of friendship or a romantic relationship with a decent fellow.

Few issues more profoundly affect our identity than what it means to be a sexual being. Abuse triggers a powerful reaction that shapes our identity, who we are. Because we live in such a sexually charged, highly experimental culture, the reality of personal shame rooted in sexual violation is increasing exponentially.

In pastoral counseling we (Steve and Sally) have spent time with many young men who had homosexual encounters at vulnerable moments in their childhood. Typically these young men had not instigated homosexual contact themselves, but they were aroused, sexualized, by the actions. Later as young adults, they wonder, "Perhaps I am a homosexual. Why else would that man or friend or older brother have chosen me? Why did I respond the way I did?"

Despite the fact that they were the victims and not the perpetrators, these young men consistently bear a profound shame that has shaped their identity. Even when the precipitating event could be identified and named ("he did that to me"), the man still thinks, "I did something to participate in this act." Often that means, "I didn't tell anybody what happened, so that means I was somehow attracted to this homosexual individual."

Most of the young men we have worked with in these cases have a desire to marry and start a family of their own, but they are haunted by the shame of events and actions that happened years before, hindering their ability to fully connect with and commit to a woman even when they deeply care for her.

Sexual abuse is deadly. So is the shame that comes from being raised in an emotionally abusive home. Neglect, ridicule, and caustic anger translate into worthlessness at the speed of light. Something in a child is quick to believe that grown-ups are always right and that the child is responsible for even the destructive choices the grown-up makes.

The most obvious form of abuse is physical abuse. But even in this realm, a child (or an adult) can feel that he or she caused the abuse by provoking the abuser. The abuser blames the victim; the victim believes that lie; and shame is woven into the victim's identity.

The tragedy doesn't stop there. Instead it sets up a self-fulfilling, cyclical tragedy. The abused one lives out his or her internal shame by making choices that increase his or her profound sense of worthlessness. Abuse is significant; don't minimize it. In the last few pages, we have only scratched the surface of this issue. If you are reading this book and know that the barb of abuse has embedded itself in your soul, this may very well be the time to ask God to help you move toward a place of healing. We encourage you to seek healing. A good place to begin is to pick up Dan Allender's book and companion workbook *The Wounded Heart*. The four of us have read it and benefited from it. No matter your past, we imagine it will help you as well.

GENDER SHAME: THE BARB OF INADEQUACY

Babies are not embarrassed by their bodies—they are oblivious to them. We laugh at a tubby little child who streaks naked through the house trying to escape his parent's summons to the bathtub, but that same behavior in an older child disturbs us. Part of maturation is the growing awareness of one's body and a corresponding desire for privacy.

Modesty has traditionally been considered a good kind of shame. We cover our bodies in the presence of others because of a healthy sense of shame and embarrassment. From the Bible's perspective the shame that produces physical modesty is a built-in component of our fallen condition—a gift from God that keeps us from inappropriate intimacy, indiscretion, and sexual sin.

However, it is altogether a different issue when modesty is an expression of inadequacy or disgust. Our culture is schizophrenic on this matter. Lithe men and women whose nakedness is hidden only by the angle of the camera abound in advertising, on magazine covers, in movies, and online. With the "beautiful people" constantly parading perfect bodies before our eyes, it is easy to believe we do not measure up. The excessive modesty that comes from gender shame is really about inadequacy.

We especially see the impact of gender shame in women's attitudes toward their bodies. How else can we explain the exploding industry of liposuction, Botox, face lifts, and breast enlargement surgeries? When we talked with a young woman named Emily, she laid out very clearly the acute power of gender shame.

At twenty-one her figure wasn't what she had hoped for. Her sister looked great in a swimsuit, but Emily hadn't bought a new one in three years. The agony of trying on twenty different suits in the hopes of finding one she could tolerate was just too great. Usually she just wore her old one and her brother's T-shirt. Or she chose not to go swimming. The magazines at the grocery-store checkout mocked her every time she stood in line. So did most of the women in the movies. Why does a girl have to be reminded of what she *isn't* every time she turns around? What else could she do but get out her credit card and make an appointment with a plastic surgeon for breast enlargements?

The shame of failing to meet standards of sexual beauty or prowess is a powerfully toxic barb for men as well. Lack of sexual accomplishment in all its forms implicates a man's very identity. When a man bears gender shame, he all too often withdraws into a world of masturbation or pornography. It is easier to find an outlet there than to expose himself to the risk of a relationship with a real person.

In men and women alike, addictions flourish when gender shame wounds the soul. Indiscrete romantic flings, voyeurism,

Internet pornography, homosexuality, frigidity, compulsive masturbation, impotence, and eating disorders all have roots in an inability to form appropriate sexual relationships—an inability fostered by gender shame.

FAMILY SHAME: THE BARB OF BEING LIKE THEM

Some families cause chronic and profound embarrassment to their members. When a father is imprisoned, the whole family suffers shame. Alcohol and drug addiction can produce generations of shame and entrapment. Mental illness can do the same. We want to hide—everyone must know that "our daddy is crazy." We feel afraid and doomed. Will we inevitably repeat our parent's or sibling's story?

When a child rebels against the norms of society, the whole family feels the stigma. A mother experiences shame when her son returns home drunk from party after party or is arrested for a DUI. A brother is shamed by the locker-room whisperings about his "loose" sister. Older people embarrass their children and their grandchildren when they fulfill demeaning stereotypes. For example, an older black woman who was put down again and again by racial prejudice may be ill at ease and deferential around a white person, but her teenage grandchild will cringe while she watches the encounter. Young people can shame their parents and grandparents by simply living in a new culture that the older generation misunderstands and rejects. As interrelated groups of people, family members cannot help but affect each other.

I (Ralph) have spent the last several years talking to a young man named Eric. Eric can't figure out how to make a decisive move toward marriage. He bears the shame of his parents' divorce and the stigma of his father's liaisons with women who are too young for him. But more than that, he fears he is doomed to repeat his father's choices. After all, he shares his genetics. And he has to own the fact that he sees in himself the all-too-obvious tendencies to continue his father's pattern of noncommitment. In his mind it is very hard to separate himself from his family. He is part of their system and therefore part of their shame.

ETHNIC SHAME: THE BARB OF WHO MY PEOPLE ARE

Ethnic shame is similar to family shame, but it is played out in a larger arena. The problem is not just with the family we are part of but with the whole culture or race that formed us or that we inhabit. Most people use the words *culture* and *race* interchangeably, but they are different. Very simply, a culture (a way of living—including communication, values, and art) can be embraced by many different races (typified mostly by genetics, especially color of skin and hair—many sociologists have concluded there is no such thing as "race" among humans, that there is only the "human race"). Sometimes a group of people has formed its own way of living among a larger group—its own subculture. And it gets more complicated from here. A more accurate description of what we normally mean by *race* and *culture* is *ethnicity*, and that is the term we shall use here when we mean both.

I (Sally) remember the first time ethnic shame hit me. I was born in the Deep South and believed throughout my childhood that the South was the best of all possible worlds. Then in the late '60s I went to college outside the world I knew, and it became immediately apparent that many people in this new world looked down on me because of my culture. Where I was from, my accent, my white skin had to mean I was an ignorant, redneck bigot. I felt the shame of "who my people are." Almost forty years later, it can still happen. I love where I am from, but in certain contexts, I would rather it not be the first thing people know about me.

That sense of being judged prematurely was my first insight into the damning, shaming power of racial prejudice. We live in a world where racial injustice is illegal, yet no one sensitive to the reality of human interactions believes that our racial issues are solved. Racial tensions simmer just below the surface in the United States, and people of color continue to live as the objects of explosive anger, taunting remarks, or prejudice. There are no easy answers to the resulting shame, even in a culture committed to racial equality.

As much as we rail against the irrational thinking of racial and cultural prejudice, we still live with it and are polluted by it. We live with the shame of what *we*, our ethnic group, have done to others, and we live with the shame of what has been done to *us*. The barb of "who my people are" flies in every direction—from the victim to the perpetrator of injustice.

When we are part of a dominant culture at a particular point in history, we are often unaware of the shame we bear for past cultural prejudice. We resist the idea that we should be ashamed. European Americans often feel no sense of shame for the atrocities their ancestors committed in the enslavement of African Americans or the near genocide of Native Americans. Others in the world community, however, are quick to condemn white Americans for both their historical behavior and for their current lack of sensitivity to past racial horrors. Efforts to rectify the problem today often backfire, and the problem of racial conflict rises like a phoenix from the bitter ashes of history. The problem does not happen only in America. World events circle around issues of shame. When a member of the dominant culture finally feels the shame of past behavior, it can be akin to discovering that your fly was open when you gave a speech — *yesterday*. Your shame backs up to cover a past you can't change.

As an African American growing up in the southern United States, Frances knew the poison of this barb and felt powerless to fight it even in a culture working to legislate corrective measures. When you are a member of an ethnic group that has been historically hated or slurred, what voice is powerful enough to tell you that what *they* say about you or what *they* do to you is not possibly the real truth? It can take years to extinguish the power of the shame that comes to us simply by being born as "one of them."

EXISTENTIAL SHAME: THE BARB OF CYNICISM

A tragic form of shame infecting our world today is the vague existential shame born from a sense of worthlessness and powerlessness. More often than not, this kind of shame removes any sense of meaning from a person and replaces it with cynicism. When our hearts are poisoned by this barb, we are convinced that our existence in this world means nothing, that the world would be a better place without us.

This personal shame is reinforced by a naturalistic or atheistic worldview that agrees with our assessment of ourselves. Humans have no uniqueness or real value; they are simply animals like the other animals on the planet. Compared to other animals, people do more damage to each other and to the environment than any of the other animals.

In a truly naturalistic worldview, no logical remedy exists to deal with how flawed we are except to eliminate our race—an idea popularized in movies such as *The Matrix*. In *The Matrix*, artificially intelligent machines that look like people lead a concerted effort to imprison the human race because, as one of them puts it, "You're not actually mammals. . . . [you're] a virus. Human beings are a disease, a cancer of this planet."[1]

As extreme as a view like this is, it filters into the psyche of the world. Pop culture, music, and art speak the same message. Young adults, especially, have taken in the message of worthlessness as no other generation. The message they hear is the bitter fruit of the beliefs of the past two centuries, which have cut us off from a sense of purpose, responsibility, and hope.

Without meaning, we become people who see ourselves as shameful, worthless creatures. We aren't even good animals—we destroy our environment, we fill our bodies with things that wreck us, we kill our young, we hoard, we seek power over others. We are an embarrassment to nature itself. Shame in all its more personal manifestations finds fertile soil in a worldview dominated by such cynicism.

As believers we may protest that feeling like this is illegitimate, that it is counter to the truth of God. But we all know people like Jonathan, a young man we interviewed, or maybe we, too, are like him.

Jonathan lives his life hounded by feelings of worthlessness. At times he has felt useful and almost buoyant, like things were beginning to fit together, but usually he's resigned to the fact that his life amounts to nothing. No matter where he looks, he can't find a purpose for life that can hold up under scrutiny. At best, life is fragmented; at worst, utterly meaningless. Most of the music he listens to and the films he watches reinforce his cynicism.

His childhood is part of the reason he sees things the way he does. His memories from those years are of constant criticism. Why take any initiative in work, in relationships, when you have been told again and again that you get it wrong, that you don't measure up? Why seek to accomplish great things when nothing really matters anyway? Self-condemnation and cynicism are the best defense against an empty world. Jonathan is a master at both and has been mastered by them.

More and more, believing in Christ does not seem to make a person immune to the pervasive cynicism and worthlessness that color our world. The message of meaninglessness is a ready-made, self-fulfilling prophecy. Not always, but often, it strips us of our desire to make a difference in this world. Why take any initiative? No matter what anybody says about work or relationships or even life itself, none of it matters. In fact, there is no reason to imagine that we really matter. If who we are and what we do amounts to nothing, why put forth much effort?

Different Types of Shame

Performance Shame	The Barb of Failure
Image Shame	The Barb of Losing Face
Victim Shame	The Barb of Abuse
Gender Shame	The Barb of Inadequacy
Family Shame	The Barb of Being Like Them
Ethnic Shame	The Barb of Who My People Are
Existential Shame	The Barb of Cynicism

WHAT DO WE DO WITH WHAT WE'VE FOUND?

Our goal in looking at these seven barbs of shame is not to dissect, label, and thereby *solve* the sense of shame we live with. Instead, we are hoping to understand where our shame comes from. The truth is, shame has a multitude of barbs. In this book we are calling these barbs "the heaped-on shame" that is put on us. And the categories of heaped-on shame go on and on.

You can probably think of barbs of shame we haven't mentioned. For example, you may be well acquainted with socioeconomic shame. This shame is not tied to your income or what you own — it's a product of how you see yourself in relationship to those who have more, or less, than you do.

Or perhaps you know the barb of religious shame. The group you are a part of has given you a sense that, spiritually speaking, you don't measure up. What you believe, eat or won't eat, wear or won't wear, do or won't do, how you worship, who you call your friends, how you vote (the list is endless) determine your place in the pecking order of what it means to be spiritual. The lower you are, the more ashamed you feel or should feel.

The barbs of shame are common to everyone. We all experience some form of shame — whether it's related to performance or identity, family or ethnicity, gender or the message of human worthlessness, how much we have or don't have, or abusive events that have happened to us. Shame has been put upon us by culture, family expectations, and religious norms. And we contribute to our own heaped-on shame — the way we see ourselves, our evaluation of our successes and our failures. All of these are "heaped-on shame."

However, the knowledge that our lives have been invaded by a few (or even several) forms of heaped-on shame is just the starting point for discussion. We have a longer, more complex journey to take — a journey to determine whether there is a difference between false heaped-on shame and what may exist at an even deeper level of the soul: true *identity-level shame.*

Often we confuse these two kinds of shame. Heaped-on shame feels like it is about us, but actually its root is in some wound or personal inadequacy. Inadequacies aren't sinful (not everyone can swim as fast as Michael Phelps), but in a world that ranks everything, our inadequacies make us feel bad about ourselves.

Identity-level shame is different. It makes us feel bad too, but it is telling us something true about ourselves. We feel bad about ourselves because we really are badly flawed by virtue of our choices and because we are Adam's children.

A journey toward our identity-level shame is not easy. Facing and feeling shame are like having major surgery. It hurts and our instinct is to avoid it, to declare that we actually don't feel that bad after all.

But if there is a difference between heaped-on shame and deserved identity-level shame, then failure to distinguish the two can be spiritually deadly. By ignoring the latter we deny a truth we all know—that some of our shame hasn't been heaped on us . . . it really does belong to us. In other words, we are on a journey to find the root of true shame that exists in us. When we find it, we need to understand it, embrace it, and hear its message.

Notice we did not say *eradicate it.* We are headed to a far different place than simply ridding ourselves of all shame. As we have seen, shame has been heaped on us in many twisted ways. But healing will not come by glibly labeling all shame as bad.

In the years spent exploring this subject, we have come to a different conclusion. We believe that we must walk into the depths of our shame and acknowledge that parts of our shame are deserved. Then and only then can we receive healing for the true root of shame, our identity-level shame. And then and only then will we find freedom from the burden of the shame that has been heaped upon us. Finding the antidote to identity-level shame loosens the grip heaped-on shame has on us. Light and freedom begin to slowly emerge.

The Scriptures themselves are our guide. In them we will see God meeting us in our shame and offering us His mercy. He takes our shame as His own through Christ on the cross, and then He exchanges our shame for His Son's beauty. Our very identity is changed. As we ponder the message of Jesus Christ and how it speaks to us, we have the opportunity to arrive at a place of profound hope and spiritual transformation.

But first we must take a deep look at what we would rather ignore and conceal—our true shame. This journey is long and difficult. You will not find the experience of total healing for your heart by the end of this book. We certainly haven't come to a place of full healing in our own battles with shame. But as we enter this dark terrain, as we accept the reality that we are flawed and helpless, we find the way to the wonderful mercy of God.

Pause to Reflect

Which types of shame do you most identity with?

How has one of these barbs of shame impacted your life? Be as specific as you can.

Pause to Listen:
Lydia's Story

Shame finds its breeding ground
in many different places. Its
power to grow and reproduce
does not depend on tragic
circumstances, years of abuse, or
homes that struggle under the weight
of severely twisted relationships.

Lydia told her story to the four of us
one night over supper. She spent her childhood
on the prairies of the Midwest, growing up in a hardworking
community of farmers scattered across the vast wheat fields.
Everyone around her was connected by blood or years of shared
history. She inherited the culture of her grandparents, who
were Russian immigrants of Germanic descent. Immigrant
children with similar roots attended the same small school and
church that she did, shared the same customs and food, used
the same expressions in their speech, and celebrated holidays
as her family did. Why did she feel so different? Why did it
matter so much? She turned to her parents for comfort, but
they were stoic people, used to harsh conditions, afraid of their
own emotions, reluctant to spoil their children by being too
tender.

Lydia's fork rested on the edge of her plate as she continued.
"I remember lying in bed at night, wishing my mother would
come to my room, sit on the edge of my bed, and rub my back

or give me a hug. I particularly remember one night when I was about six or seven. We didn't tell each other 'I love you' in our family, but I wanted so badly to say it to my mother. I prayed she would come into the room to check on me, but she never did things like that. Finally I just had to go tell her. I heard her door close and knew she was on her way to bed. So I ran in and threw my arms around her. I buried my whole face against her. 'I love you,' I blurted out.

"Do you know what she did?" Lydia looked around at us as she asked the question. "Mom gave me a quick hug and a little shove. 'Don't be silly,' she said. 'Get back to bed.'"

Lydia shrugged and went on. When she was nine, her aunt encouraged her to go to a Christian summer camp, and it was there she began her relationship with Christ. Her conversion has protected her in many ways from trying to find love and acceptance in all the wrong ways. "But," she said, "the feeling of being different and unloved was still there."

When Lydia was in her early teens, her family moved to a nearby town. The opportunity to leave the confines of life on the farm excited her. Maybe now life would be easier; maybe she would be understood. She did well—she made friends and good grades, but her image of herself as the misfit farm girl could not be erased. Even in the twelfth grade, despite the fact that she had studied the other girls almost as intensely as she had studied her schoolwork, she still felt different from them all. And different was bad. There was no category for "good differences" in this small town—a fact that was driven home to her more than once.

All four of us know Lydia, know that she chose a career path landing her in a respected, visible profession geared toward helping others. We know that she has done well. But as we listened that night, we heard a different slant on her success story.

Early in Lydia's career, something surfaced that surprised and shamed her even more than being different and misunderstood. She is naturally a good listener, and people easily open their souls to her. It is part of her gifting and part of her work. People come to her for advice, for friendship, for comfort. But as her skills and reputation grew, Lydia found herself dismayed rather than encouraged—she realized these skills that enabled her to be so effective in her work had also enabled her to hide her true self from others and herself.

It felt good to be the one people confided in. The "bad" differences that had lingered since childhood faded away while she was in session with a client. But it also felt terrible. Who was she really, deep down? She still felt so different. Did that mean she was wrong or flawed? What would it do to her own soul to hide behind her ability to help others for a lifetime? Did she need to feel accepted to be okay?

Lydia finished her story, and her questions hung in the air unanswered. The truth is, she is an accomplished woman. She is the first person in her family to further her education past high school. She has affirmation all around her that she is a compassionate, wise, spiritual person. She desires to deal honestly with herself and with others. But on some level her personal misgivings remain. Is she worse than the ignorant, little immigrant girl? Has she traded naiveté for something far worse?

Perhaps you know the power of Lydia's questions. What do you do with your shame when all the people in your world count on you to be wise and competent and compassionate?

What do you do when you feel trapped by their good opinion of you?

CHAPTER THREE

True Roots and
Faulty Tactics

In the last chapter, we introduced a very challenging course of action. Choosing to explore our identity-level shame—the shame that is rightfully ours because of our choices and because of our heritage as children of Adam—is painful. Instinctively, we want to label all shame as bad and say that it came from outside of ourselves. As tragic as it may be when others heap shame on us and as much as we may want to say "my shame is a result of *their* words and actions," the barbs of heaped-on shame are always looking for ways to embed themselves in our souls. However, the identity-level shame we bear is not just anecdotal and random; it is not just foisted upon us. Rather it's symptomatic of who we are. It's as if our souls have gigantic yellow, black, and red targets drawn on them, and the nasty words and unjust attitudes shot our way often hit the bull's-eye that we provide.

On some level every one of us walks around with a sense of worthlessness, of not measuring up, of being flawed or power-less to change. We feel worthless because the truth is, at our core each of us is deeply flawed. This sounds like an insensitive statement, especially to people struggling under the burden of heaped-on shame. But take a look at how God evaluates all of us. In Romans 3:10-14, He pulls no punches:

> There is no one righteous, not even one;
> > there is no one who understands,
> > no one who seeks God.
> All have turned away,
> > *they have together become worthless;*
> there is no one who does good,
> > not even one.
> Their throats are open graves;
> > their tongues practice deceit.
> The poison of vipers is on their lips.
> > Their mouths are full of cursing and bitterness.
> > (emphasis added)

We might try to squirm out from under this assessment by arguing that it is just our actions that have made us worthless, that in the core of who we *are*, we are okay. But as we keep checking out what the Bible has to say, we discover it gives a different perspective. Job, one of the wisest men of the ancient world, confessed,

> I am afraid of all my pains,
> I know that You will not acquit me.
> I am accounted wicked,
> Why then should I toil in vain?
> If I should wash myself with snow
> And cleanse my hands with lye,
> Yet You would plunge me into the pit. (9:28-31, NASB)

To acknowledge the reality of who we really are, we need to let the hard truths of the Scriptures speak to us. Other passages describe the state of our souls in far more graphic terms. For example, in Ezekiel 16:4-5, God allegorically spoke to His chosen people with startling imagery:

> On the day you were born your cord was not cut . . . nor were you rubbed with salt or wrapped in cloths. No one looked . . . with pity or had compassion enough to do any of these things for you. Rather, you were thrown out into the open field, for on the day you were born you were despised.

The text goes on to detail how Israel, rescued from the trash heap and made beautiful by God, chose degradation far worse than her birth origins. Looking at His opening salvo, we realize that God was speaking to the people of Israel not about the degradation their choices had brought upon themselves but about *who they were at the time of their birth.* He was talking about their identity—from birth they were abandoned, ugly, rejected, and despised. Furthermore, this is a description of God's chosen people, not a description of the nations and cultures that openly rejected Him.

Can this raw assessment really be true? Does it apply to us as well? Are we so lacking in worth, in desirability, that we matter as little as a baby abandoned in a dumpster? Is our ancestry so low that we lack even simple human dignity? If this is really the way God feels about us, how can there ever be any hope? If we take to heart what we are hearing, disturbing questions emerge.

Some of us are aware of these possibilities without any help from the passage in Ezekiel. Remember Dan, the young man I (Steve) had coffee with? The one who said, "You just don't understand. There's something wrong with *me.* I feel like crap. In fact, I *am* crap!" A current of shame ran like a powerful and dangerous undertow through his soul. You may be like him—able to fully recount the truth of the gospel, but your shame is still there, resistant to logic and argument.

Where do emotions like this come from? Are they heaped on us by life and people? Do they arise because we really haven't believed the good news? Really haven't committed ourselves to

Christ? Or is it possible that these sorts of emotions do have true things to tell us about ourselves?

God seems to think so. His words through Paul, Job, and Ezekiel all indicate that something is wrong with us. People experience different barbs of heaped-on shame, and they feel the pain of their identity-level shame to varying degrees. None of us is entirely free from the disturbing sense that we are not okay.

But where does it come from? In other words, what is the root of identity-level shame?

THE ROOT OF OUR IDENTITY-LEVEL SHAME

The human heart has not always known shame. At the beginning of creation, shame was a stranger, an unknown experience. Commenting on the two people God had made, the writer of Genesis said, "The man and his wife were both naked, and they felt no shame" (2:25).

If you went to Sunday school as a child and heard the creation story, you may remember reacting differently to these words than you did to other verses in the Bible. Adam and Eve went around all day with their clothes off? You mean they never even wore any? As a child you possibly felt what I (Steve) did, a sense of both giggly embarrassment and awe. You're not supposed to go around naked, but then what would a world be like where you didn't feel bad about being naked? What would a world be like where other people could see everything about you, and you would still be okay?

Adam and Eve's nakedness did not just play itself out on a physical stage. They lived out of soul nakedness as well. Whatever they did, whatever they felt, the other could know and God knew—all without shame. There was nothing to shield from view. That's very different from the world we live in.

Even in our world, with its flagrant displays of the human body, its nude beaches, its graphic magazines (freely accessible to any preteen at the grocery-store checkout), and its countless X-rated Internet sites we can look at in the secrecy of our homes, we still know intuitively that unrestricted physical exposure is inappropriate. Clothing is a necessary protection from eyes that do not need to see our uncovered bodies. Nakedness is without shame only in a limited number of settings. Otherwise something about it is embarrassing, humiliating, degrading. In spite of the efforts of current Western society to make it "good," unrestricted exposure is not fun, free, and natural.

Many would consider this statement restrictive or outdated in our take-it-all-off society. Before you dismiss it, however, wrestle with a couple of thoughts. Professional marriage counselors tell us that many women cannot undress in front of their own husbands because of an overwhelming sense of shame. Or consider your reactions to the black-and-white photographs of naked prisoners on their way to extermination at the Nazi concentration camps. Their plight is made even more degrading by their forced nakedness. Your reaction to these photos is not just cultural; it is rooted in your soul. Physical exposure against our wills means more than just flesh; it means our souls are in clear view. Deep down we sense there is something we need to hide. We don't want the world to see all of us anytime it chooses. Instinctively we need the right and freedom to cover ourselves.

So what's changed since the days when Adam and Eve walked around naked and free, without shame and with nothing to hide? They were given tremendous freedom, responsibility, dignity, and opportunity in an open, dynamic relationship with God. God never designed that relationship to be robotic or dutiful. He wanted this first couple to freely engage with Him — not out of fear or coercion but because they loved Him. Giving them the dignity of choice, He included one prohibition in the equation: an opportunity for them to choose to love God by deferring to that prohibition. Adam and Eve chose independence from God even as they sought to become "like God" (Genesis 3:5).

Their fatal decision catapulted the whole human race into a new kind of existence. God had promised that disobedience would bring death. Their rejection of the one limit God had placed on their lives meant they were instantly and objectively guilty, and that guilt was coupled with another equally objective reality: spiritual separation and death. The story in Genesis 3 indicates they felt the guilt and separation from God — and that "felt guilt" became the headwaters of shame for the whole human race. They were objectively guilty, *and* they felt ashamed for what they had done and who they had become. Objective guilt became subjective shame, which infiltrated their actions and their beings.

In the intricate web that exists between body and spirit,

Adam and Eve's response to their exposed bodies became a mirror by which they could see the condition of their souls. Their eyes were opened: They saw they were naked, and they felt ashamed because of it. Shame was a new response to the nakedness they had formerly participated in with such freedom, and they sewed fig leaves together to cover themselves — hiding themselves from God and each other. The point we must not forget is this: They felt ashamed because of what they had done wrong, and that wrongdoing altered their souls and their world forever.

Guilt opened a Pandora's box of shame and its bitter fruit. Shame became embedded in our identity. But unlike Adam and Eve, we often cannot point to a specific sin we committed to explain the shame. It is just there. So our shame leads us to a spiritual reality that came into being at the fall of man — something is wrong with us. We are fundamentally flawed. We all feel the need to hide. From this vantage point we can begin to understand the harsh indictments from Romans 3 and Ezekiel 16 that relate to our deepest identity.

We need to consider something further before moving on. Adam and Eve are the only people in history whose sinful actions preceded a shamefulness that was not there before. Since then all of us have been born with sin and the seeds of shame. What they did to the human race is akin to altering a genetic code; every subsequent generation bears the altered gene.

In Psalm 51, David spoke for the whole human race: "I was brought forth in iniquity, and in sin my mother conceived me" (verse 5, NASB). The problem is in our spiritual DNA. To put it bluntly, we are ashamed because we are sinners. Because of what Adam and Eve did, we are sinners even before we sin. The Bible's message about our spiritual condition is that we have a problem with sin (the defining principle of our being) before we have a problem with sins (the actions we do).

Jesus said it directly:

> Do you not understand that everything that goes into the mouth passes into the stomach, and is eliminated? But the things that proceed out of the mouth come from the heart, and those defile the man. For out of the heart come evil thoughts, murders, adulteries, fornications, thefts, false witness, slanders. These are the things which defile the man. (Matthew 15:17-20, NASB)

The deepest source of our problems is not what we do (and what comes to us from others) but who we are. That reality of inborn sin traps our lives in shame from which we have no human escape.

In our efforts to affirm the essential value of every human being, the concept of spiritual twistedness seems psychologically fatal. We shout against such a notion: "No! Every person is valuable. Every person is good and beautiful inside." Or we take it even further. According to some belief systems, humans have a spark of divinity that needs only to be fanned into flame.

But most people still want to understand why they cannot easily shake their deep sense of shame; they understand (by conviction or intuition) what G. K. Chesterton called easily the most provable doctrine from the Bible, the basic sinfulness of humanity.[1]

But even those of us who admit to the "basic sinfulness of humanity" cast about for an escape hatch—some point of dignity, some proof of innate worth and beauty. It is hard to submit to what the Scriptures declare: We are born in a state of sin, and that sin inevitably produces shame (see Psalm 51:5). The point is that our efforts to deny those shameful origins actually cut us off from the only cure offered for the real disease.

As the four of us discussed our own battles with shame, it became clear that each of us had developed fairly sophisticated methods for hiding our shame from ourselves and others. As serious and sincere followers of Jesus Christ, we had even Christianized our hiding mechanisms. So we decided to be frank with each other and do our best to expose these strategies.

God's Word helped us as we faced the hide-and-seek games we play to ignore, disguise, and run from our shame. God knows we are all game players, and His record of human stories is very candid. The Bible exposes the spiritual and emotional strategies people adopt to deny and cover the shame inside.

For the rest of this chapter as well as in chapter 4, we'll take a look at some of those strategies. We imagine you will find some of your own methodologies for hiding your shame in the following sections. You will also read some of the strategies and say, "I never do that." Fair enough. But watch for the ones you do use.

GRAB THE FIG LEAVES

One of the most basic strategies for dealing with shame goes back to the pattern established by our original parents. Adam and Eve reacted to their sudden exposure by covering up their physical nakedness. Apparently they hoped that physical coverings could deal with spiritual shame. We do the same. We know we're flawed, but instead of asking for a solution from God, whom we have offended, we try to look good, projecting a beautiful image. We concentrate on posturing, shifting the focus from ourselves by blaming others, pointing out their nakedness while desperately reaching for the fig-leaf costume hanging in our own closet.

There are infinite ways to cover up our internal struggles with external appearances. Religious habits and words, beauty, wealth, academic prowess, rough-and-tumble masculinity, iconoclastic eccentricity—the list goes on. We are masters of fig-leafism.

To change the metaphor, we pull out the bucket and brush and paint ourselves beautiful like the Pharisees, who Jesus indicted in Matthew 23. Jesus reserved His most scathing denunciations for these religious leaders who proclaimed themselves experts on truth yet utterly failed to know the God of truth. Their right doctrine did not touch their hearts. In verse 27, Jesus exposed them: "Woe to you, teachers of the law and Pharisees, you hypocrites! You are like whitewashed tombs, which look beautiful on the outside but on the inside are full of dead men's bones and everything unclean."

In a world that prized religion, the Pharisees were experts in presenting a hyper-religiosity. They looked beautiful, but their beauty was nothing more than whitewash—watered-down paint that barely covered the ugly blemishes infecting their souls.

Andrew Lloyd Webber took the story of Eva Perón and created the powerful musical *Evita*, which explores the passions of a woman determined to maintain an image of beauty and power. Desperate to cover up her low-class background and illegitimate birth, Evita is a prototype of the social climber.

In the end, ravaged by incurable cancer, she was unable to accept the love of her husband because she simply couldn't believe that a person could love someone who was not beautiful, powerful, or productive. She spent her life looking good on the outside, and when the image crumbled, her emptiness was revealed. She managed never to let anyone, not even her adoring husband, touch the hidden darkness of her soul.

Whether or not *Evita* is historically correct, we know from firsthand experience that it accurately depicts our desperate attempts to maintain an external image at all costs. Whatever the ethos of our particular culture or society, we learn to play the image game early in life. We are masters at it, able to incorporate shifting definitions of success into our image in a heartbeat, projecting and posing in different settings so that no matter what the game is, we can always come out "looking good."

For example, the culture of the '90s valued honesty over virtue, so we had public figures *honestly* proclaiming their immorality, appealing to us to respect them for the fact that they finally had come out of whatever closet they'd been hiding in. No matter if what they were honestly declaring was morally repugnant or clearly illegal, the image of honesty carried the day.

The fig-leaf strategy of "pretend and hide" becomes deeply entrenched in our hearts. I (Steve) knew a couple for several years who always seemed to be on top of the world. Life was wonderful, according to them; a quick smile and "Praise the Lord!" covered every difficulty. Several times in the beginning of our relationship Sally and I went to them for advice. Their response never varied: Life could be wonderful if you had enough faith and if you obeyed God. It was pretty obvious, to them and to me, that I must not be measuring up because my life was not a juggernaut of unblemished success. So I plugged away, trying to have enough faith and always do the right thing.

I particularly remember one night at a small dinner party; we had just returned from a vacation with Sally's family. I asked the husband if he had ever struggled with getting along with his father-in-law. Trying to sew my own fig leaves, I made what I considered to be an astute remark for a man just thirty-two years old: "It's hard for two heads of household to be in the same house for too long."

I can still hear his response. He looked at me solemnly and then declared, "I have never had any problems getting along with my in-laws."

"Never?" I queried.

"Never," he said emphatically, looking at me as if there were no way I could be his pastor (which I was) and probably no way I could be a Christian man.

And then his wife chirped in, "There's always been so much love in our family, and Martin has been just like a son to my dad."

As Christians twenty years their junior, Sally and I marveled (but also felt a solid load of shame). They were so together; we so obviously weren't. But something still niggled at the back of my mind. I wasn't sure I really believed them. On the other hand, from what they said, they enjoyed a very different life from the one we were experiencing.

The bubble began to burst when this family faced a serious combination of crises. They entered into a period of job uncertainty and economic stress. But "everything was still fine." Then the husband was diagnosed with a serious, life-threatening illness. Everything was still "fine." Then they were hit with what seemed to be an over-the-top tragedy. Their son, whom they loved and prized, abandoned his faith, his wife, and his children for a series of other women.

Assuming they would naturally be heartbroken over his actions, we went to see them, hoping to provide some camaraderie and comfort. In that conversation at their kitchen table, as we asked what seemed to be normal questions about how they were handling the challenges, we were surprised to hear that they were still "fine."

Then they spoke these unforgettable words: "Looking back, we can't think of one thing—*one thing*—we ever did wrong or one thing we should have done differently as parents."

It is true that an adult child makes his own decisions and cannot blame his parents for his foolishness. But what parent can honestly say, "I can't think of one thing I ever did wrong or one thing that I'd do differently"? Denial had become a way of life, and the fig leaves never came off.

I doubt we ever fully outgrow our fig-leafing tendencies. Heaven alone will be our place of healing, where all the veils and cover-ups will be removed and Christ will expose each person's life for what it is. He alone has the power to bring all things into conformity with His nature (see Philippians 3:21). Only then will our transformation be complete and our fig leaves all fall off and wither away.

In the meantime, we battle to be honest. For example, I (Steve) live in a world where aggressive, decisive leadership and sharp strategic thinking are valued. I must confess that I enjoy a roundtable of people attacking a strategic problem and the key insight or question coming from—you guessed it—yours truly. I find myself working hard to put on the appearance of strategic competence. That's what my world values, and I want to make sure that I look the part even if I'm completely clueless as to what to do in a given situation.

Many of the people around me value relationships and love, and I realized recently that I am often far more concerned with *looking like* a loving person than with actually loving the people in my life. I find myself worrying about whether or not I have done the loving thing and whether or not the people around me have noticed how loving I am. Such a strategy of projecting and posing is a far cry from actually loving and enjoying a person.

In other words, all too often I find myself working on my

fig-leaf costume rather than loving my wife, children, and friends. I have found myself more satisfied when I "did the right thing by telephoning a struggling friend" than when my friend actually gained victory in his struggle.

What is the image of success embodied in your culture, your family, your profession, or your community? How do you work to make sure you project the right image regardless of whether or not you embody the reality?

If the values behind the image are good biblical values (love, for instance), how are you seeking to become the person you are determined to be versus looking like the person you are expected to be? How do you respond when you come close to the burn of shame in your heart? Do you run to the closet and look for the latest suit of fig leaves?

BUILD ME A WALL

Another ancient strategy for dealing with our shame is to build a wall of protection around our souls. If others can't see what's inside of us, perhaps we won't have to acknowledge it either.

Indeed, when it comes to strategies for avoiding shame, there is nothing new under the sun. In Ezekiel 13 God rebuked the false prophets and said that He would tear down the whitewashed walls they had built and expose the foundation. God is not against all walls. The book of Nehemiah tells the story of rebuilding the wall around Jerusalem. It's a story of strength and courage and the goodness of hard work done in obedience to God. Good walls and good boundaries protect us from danger. But in our desire to hide, we can also build false walls, whitewash them so they are pleasing, and then spend our lives hiding behind them.

Perhaps the best way to tell whether you are heavily invested in the wrong kind of wall-building is to listen to the reflections of a young woman. She realized that wall-building had been her strategy of choice, but she also saw that her walls were taking life from her instead of giving life to her. With her permission, we quote a letter she wrote:

> Thank you again for your time last week. I really enjoy talking to you, and I think it's even better for me than I thought it would be.
>
> The thing that really popped into my head was that I don't like to admit that I feel shame, because feeling shame would mean that I was not "over" the things that made me feel angry and shameful, and I need to insist that I am not angry. It's a weird thing to be prideful about. So many people seem to have a hang-up with having a right to righteous anger, and here my hang-up is with not having a right, not wanting anything to do with it, even if that means I sweep it under the rug and just fake like I'm over it until I actually (think I) am.
>
> To realize that you don't just forgive once is pretty new for me, and sort of a shock because I am uncovering the places where I'm still emotionally raw, still angry

and scared. Also, I don't know why I didn't think of this last week, but it is so clear to me now where a big part of my wall-building is coming from, and it's sort of a no-brainer when I think of it.

I had a falling-out with two very close friends . . . and it still makes me shake when I think of how badly I wanted things to just be normal again, and how confused and abandoned and needy I felt. I blamed myself before I blamed my friends, because I thought . . . if the friendship would not have been tested to its breaking point, and if it was never tested, I would never have to know what I couldn't count on them for. I remember thinking to myself that I must never let anyone get to me like that again, never make another friend I couldn't bear to lose.

It's worth noting that my approach to most every relationship is and has always been a very strange defensive stance, which is that I am a completely open book so long as no one reads between the lines. Like, here's the facts, but don't ask me for the truth. So people commend my honesty and call me brave (and basically I get to be the Tin Man, the Scarecrow, and the Lion all at once, plus the Good Witch too), and all the time I know that they are only getting half the story, and it's not the half that matters. So I am basically being untruthful, even though I "never" lie, and to every untrained eye I look like I am revealing everything there is to know.

I rattle off a litany of the horrible things my mother did, deadpan and with no anger in my voice, and I say I am over it: Wow, I'm so forgiving. I tell women about how I survived rape, and I say I'm not a survivor because it isn't something I live with every day; it's over, just over, and I went beyond surviving, I healed: Wow, I'm so honest. None of these things are untrue, but they are certainly not the whole truth. And I know that every person I talk to doesn't need the whole truth, but if I am going to go this far, then why not just admit that I actually experience human emotions?

I hope that makes sense to you and isn't too . . . too. I think I live in my head too much and when the words actually make it out into the world, they don't look the same as they did inside. I also hope that it's information you can use to call me out when I am telling you the facts and not the truth. I'm sure that I will do it from time to time just out of habit, and I'm being arrogant in assuming that I haven't already, because I probably have. And whether I have or not, I am sorry, because even if I didn't I probably had every intention of doing so.

You are brilliant at reading between the lines, though, so I have a feeling you either already know this about me, or it doesn't much matter because you can get past my smoke screen without too much trouble. Still, I shouldn't even have a smoke screen, especially one so elaborate and pointless. It's not like getting past it earns you a prize, and I don't see now that I have anything to gain from it, either.

Do you hear the sound of a wall being dismantled? It's a scary sound but a very good one. It opens us up to God, who is our best hope for true healing.

CRY FOR A MOUNTAIN

In Revelation 6 John painted a disturbing prophetic picture of the end of history when God the Judge unleashes terror on the world.

I watched as he opened the sixth seal. There was a great earthquake. The sun turned black like sackcloth made of goat hair, the whole moon turned blood red, and the stars in the sky fell to earth, as late figs drop from a fig tree when shaken by a strong wind. The sky receded like a scroll, rolling up, and every mountain and island was removed from its place.

Then the kings of the earth, the princes, the generals, the rich, the mighty, and every slave and every free man hid in caves and among the rocks of the mountains. They called to the mountains and the rocks, "Fall on us and hide us from the face of him who sits on the throne and from the wrath of the Lamb! For the great day of their wrath has come, and who can stand?" (Revelation 6:12-17)

On that terrible day in the future when God judges this world, many people will embrace destruction rather than cry out to God for mercy. Not wanting to face their Creator Judge, they will seek to be buried in death, crushed by the weight of darkness. They will believe the final lie that it's hopeless. Then they will cry out for a mountain to annihilate them so their shame can remain hidden.

Friends of ours (Ralph and Jennifer) had a dearly loved daughter who spent years traveling a dark, evil road, impervious to the compassion her family poured upon her. Dressed and made-up in black, with piercings all over her body, she entered into a cult of darkness and embraced a worldview of cynicism and death. Self-mutilation increased from infrequent cuts on legs and arms to regular, systematic attempts to inflict pain on herself.

Her parents could not get through to her how much they loved her. It was like pouring water on granite. She would never allow the internal shame she so heavily bore and so fiercely felt to be brought into the light. She shielded herself from the opportunity to respond to merciful love and instead sought the judgment she was sure she deserved. In a strange twist of logic, she avoided shame by embracing self-inflicted judgment.

This girl is not unusual. Take a walk through the mall.

Tune in to the conversation of kids as they wait in line at the movie theater. Go stand in a music store and read the covers of the CDs. Listen to the music.

Where does the self-hatred and despair come from? The fascination with darkness? We can't blame it all on cynicism or despair over this fragile world we live in, where every terror imaginable crouches about us. Something darker is going on. Far too many of our youth cry for a mountain in the form of dress, music, or self-mutilation; anorexia and bulimia, alcohol and drug abuse; apathy and antipathy toward their own future; violence. The shame within is rarely identified as shame, but it is there, persuading them that "life sucks" and that they can't do anything about it or about who they are.

As we've said before, shame is the normal response when a human being, created to connect profoundly and personally with God, loses touch with Him. We are cut off at the roots. Our innate desires become skewed. Something truly is wrong with us, and we feel it. Since Adam and Eve, every human being has been born in that state of disconnect.

God doesn't rush in to take the feeling away. He really can't take it away without unmaking us because shame is meant to draw us to God. Tragically, however, some people prefer judgment and destruction rather than the deep healing of God's truth and love. But running from the truth about who we are, even seeking self-condemnation, will not remove our indictment before God.

Calling for a mountain is a final defiance against God. Nevertheless, for some it is a preferred choice. In an act that marries pride to hopelessness, those who call for a mountain embrace the great delusion that darkness is all-powerful.

To summarize these first three strategies we adopt to cover our shame, fig-leafism is about posing, wall-building is about protecting, and calling for a mountain is an intense form of self-pity. In your own life, you have quite possibly (like each one of us) found yourself fairly skillful at all three. But if you don't see yourself in these strategies, there are other ways of hiding in the face of our shame. In the next chapter we'll take a look at more subtle and complex ways of dealing with the shame that creeps into all our souls.

Pause to Reflect

How would you describe the difference between heaped-on shame and identity-level shame?

Where in your life have you felt the power of heaped-on shame? Of identity-level shame?

In your own experience, do they intertwine so that it is often hard to sort them out? If so, sit for a while with your most recent experience of feeling shame. What do you think was really going on?

The three strategies in this chapter are very different from each other. Which of these three methodologies is your most likely default?

CHAPTER FOUR

Facing More Faulty Tactics

As we've seen in the previous chapter, we are resourceful people when it comes to hiding our shame. We adopt the basic strategies of posing, protecting, and pitying ourselves, and we add our unique twist to each. After all, who wants to be *obvious* about hiding from his or her shame? Of course, there are more than three ways to hide from shame. In this chapter we will look at five more strategies—building my own city, carving a cistern, spreading my skirt, doing a feel-good God-thing, and making a god like me. These strategies often take advantage of our good longings and strengths—for instance, the good drive to build something. However, we can take that which is good and develop it into a subtle strategy to cover our shame. As this chapter proceeds, it may seem that we are all caught in our shame with no place to hide. That is the place we need to be before we look at finding God's mercy and freedom from shame in subsequent chapters.

BUILD MY OWN CITY

We also cover and deny our shame by actual achievements and accomplishments. God created us in His image, which includes the capacity and responsibility to work. But many of us twist that calling and fall into patterns of overachievement and over-work. We believe we can deny our innate shamefulness by pointing to all we achieve. (If nothing else, we can ignore any feelings of shame by staying too busy to feel them.)

The story of Cain is revealing; like him, we build our own cities, monuments to human achievement, hoping to silence the voice of shame. His story unfolds in Genesis 4. He brought an offering to God that was deemed unacceptable while his brother Abel's sacrifice met God's approval. Cain responded with anger. He didn't change his offering—instead he hatched a plot to murder Abel.

God tried to help Cain with his rage, but Cain persisted and finally did his brother in. His deed brought him under God's judgment. Cain was a farmer, yet God declared that the ground would not yield its produce to his efforts and that he would be a vagrant and wanderer. Cain's response is a fascinating revelation of his heart—he rejected his judgment as unfair and distanced himself from God. Listen to his words: "My punishment is more than I can bear. Today you are driving me from the land, and I will be hidden from your presence" (verses 13-14).

What he said was not true. God never declared that He was inaccessible to Cain—that was Cain's wrong interpretation. Cain quickly learned to think, talk, and act like a victim. Fearing and mistrusting the people around him, Cain then added, "I will be a restless wanderer on the earth, and whoever finds me will kill me" (verse 14), an interesting complaint from the mouth of the first man to commit murder.

In response, God graciously drew a boundary of protection around Cain by proclaiming severe judgment on anyone who would take his life, but Cain still rejected God's restrictions on his life. He refused to acknowledge his sin or his guilt. He left God's presence, determined *not* to be a wanderer. He settled in the wilderness and constructed a city that he named after his own son, Enoch.

From this city, Cain's descendents devoted themselves to developing human culture—music, a burgeoning agricultural industry, and metalworking. Cain did everything he could to overturn God's declarations about his spiritual condition through human achievement. When God said, "You'll be a wanderer," Cain built a settled city for himself and his progeny. When God said, "The ground itself will resist you," Cain determined to make a living through ranching, mining, and metallurgy.

The point of the story is *not* that human achievements are necessarily wrong and always an attempt to avoid shame. God made us in His image—creative and expansive—and He entrusts to us the task of tending and cultivating the earth and its resources. The issue of Cain's city-building was that he embraced achieving and accomplishing as a substitute for facing his own sin and shame. When that is our tactic, no matter what we build, we are ultimately avoiding God and the healing He alone can bring.

Cain substituted achievement for authenticity. He is an archetype of the person who uses accomplishments to run from God and His declaration of our shamefulness. It does not work. God declared that Cain would be a wanderer and a vagrant—someone who could not settle or produce. Cain's defiant successes did nothing to negate that word of judgment. To the end he remained a wanderer and a vagrant—*spiritually*. Cain never settled his issues with God, so he never really settled. He was a vagrant—always a user, never a giver. He fathered a multigenerational family that never turned their hearts toward God.

No matter how beautiful the buildings of Enoch, no matter how exquisite the sounds of music wafting from its open windows, no matter how many war machines were forged in its fires, Cain is remembered for one thing and one thing only. He committed fratricide, a shameful act. Then he rejected his one hope of a cure, substituting human achievement for spiritual reality. He denied his shame, and as a result, he died in it.

Elise, an acquaintance of Sally's, recently spent two years at a prestigious graduate school. Her goal was to gain acceptance into a doctoral program at a prestigious university in England or Scotland. In her most honest moments, she knew that a longing for public achievement and recognition fueled much of her academic passion. Yes, she had a desire to make a meaningful contribution with her life, but beyond that something deep within her needed the affirmation from others that she was indeed a success.

At the beginning, everything unfolded according to plan. Elise aced every course and received an offer from her favorite professor to be his teaching assistant. Then she began to struggle with the planning of her master's thesis. Proposal after proposal was rejected. Her professor retired, leaving her in the hands of his colleague. But the colleague was not impressed with her work. "I think you'd better give up thoughts of a PhD," this new adviser told her. "Your ability won't carry you that far."

Elise had always felt like education was the path to really being somebody, but she discovered that, at best, you can only build a shaky city with your accomplishments. She has managed to get her master's degree, but she is still struggling. Her humiliation runs deep; rather than pursue a doctorate, she plans to just get a job and try to forget the whole thing.

It's been a tough journey, but Elise is facing the reality that any city we attempt to build for ourselves can be toppled by the storms of life. Those of us who stand on the sidelines of her spiritual journey see something that Elise doesn't yet see in herself. In facing her shame, no longer obsessively trying to

overcome it by accomplishments, she is being spiritually transformed—she is softer, more approachable, and more deeply
joyful. In the past, an encounter with Elise was an encounter with a driven woman. Now it is more of a reflection of
Matthew 5:3—"Blessed are the poor in spirit, for theirs is the
kingdom of heaven."

The world is filled with monuments to greatness. How
much of it was birthed from the sheer love of creativity, the
good desire to express the image of God by fashioning and
filling this world with beauty and purpose? How much of it
comes from a genuine desire to bless others? How much of it
is a passion to prove that we are great people? It would be fool-
hardy to write off all human achievement as a superficial healing for shame, as a way of avoiding our own sinful hearts. But
still we have to ask, especially in a culture as driven as ours,
what is our effort all about?

CARVE A CISTERN

In Jeremiah 2, God unleashed His indictment concerning the
spiritual apostasy of the people of Israel. His words were neither calm nor measured. God the friend, the benefactor, the
lover had been spitefully rejected. His pain was as deep and
enraged as that of a betrayed husband:

> Be appalled at this, O heavens,
>   and shudder with great horror . . .
> My people have committed two sins:

They have forsaken me,
> the spring of living water,
and have dug their own cisterns,
> broken cisterns that cannot hold water. (verses 12-13)

At the core of our beings we have a spiritual neediness rooted in the fact that we were born separated from God. We are empty people—hungry, thirsty, and unsatisfied in our spirits. We are impoverished spiritual beggars holding out empty hands that often falter as we try to receive, even from God Himself. And we will do just about anything to get rid of the feeling of spiritual emptiness. Like the people of Israel, we carve our own cisterns in an attempt to fill that void.

Cistern-carving is different than city-building. Cain sought achievements that would deny the indictment of his shamefulness, proving he had it all together. When we carve our own cisterns, we do not deny that we are thirsty; we simply try to fill the emptiness on our own without going to the source of true, living water. Like the Jews of Jeremiah's day, we forsake God and try to find our own blessings. Attempts to satisfy our hunger and thirst seem necessary and even right. We can't go through life lonely and dissatisfied, so it is only logical to meet the need any way we can. As a result, the stories that speak to our souls often are stories of cistern-carving—we identify with them.

Again, consider Evita: As an illegitimate daughter of a middle-class man and a peasant mother, she lived in poverty with her mother, rejected by her father's family. Being poor was shameful. Having a father who not would claim her as his own was shameful. But succumbing to the shame was an unbearable option. Evita found a way to overcome it and fill up her own soul. Che, the musical's narrator, describes Evita's efforts as "hustling and fighting, scratching and biting." Evita did whatever it took to fill up her cistern with adoration, beauty, and power so that her shame no longer pained her. To achieve that end, she exploited her body, her talents, and the lives of other people.

Our efforts may look polite and cultured, even spiritual, compared to Evita's, but we are after the same thing. Even as followers of Christ we want a world where our hearts are made full without the pain of waiting on God or submitting to His ways. In the end, even when our cisterns crack and we're reduced to licking up drops of dirty water, at least it's *our* cistern, the one *we* made. And we try to convince ourselves "I'm not so poor: Look at what I built for myself! I'm satisfied! I'm not thirsty anymore!"

Evita built a cistern that seemed to work. She had beauty, wealth, power, and the adoration of the masses. But even at the top, her cistern full, the cracks were already showing. Che asks Evita the question none of us wants to face: "Where do you go from here?" No cistern we build ever feels like enough. Our hunger remains; our thirst is not quenched. Evita moved from man to man, seeking someone of greater and greater prominence. When she arrived at the top of the heap as the first lady of Argentina, her thirst remained unquenched. Would recognition in Europe help? Would running the European upper class out of Argentina bring her peace? Would large-scale deeds of charity settle her soul? No resolution came, and her quest for the perfect cistern was cut short by a premature death. Our cisterns are no different. Eventually they begin to leak and inevitably run dry.

I (Steve) know one man who spent his early-adult life building his cistern — fast-rolling, high-stakes finances, living on credit in hopes of future deals, always looking for a bigger and better cash cow. He was after adventure.

Adventure in itself is not a bad thing. God has hardwired a desire for it into our psyches, and He actually wants to give us adventure as we wholeheartedly follow Him. But my friend wasn't too concerned about *that* kind of adventure when he started his run.

He pursued it all — exotic travel, incredible wealth, first-class anything and everything, relationships with high rollers — and for a while he got it. At times his life sounded like an action-hero script. A solid commitment to gambling big at everything, always hoping for a streak of luck, meant he walked the edge of a financial precipice. He made and lost enough money to float half a dozen families for life (that's not hyperbole — it's a fact!) in his efforts to fill the emptiness inside. It didn't work. He hit the wall of bankruptcy, and the empire crashed down.

Suddenly he was forced to face the cracks in his cistern and found himself licking the bottom of a well gone dry. But even if it had all worked, he would have had to come to terms with boredom. And in that boredom, the restlessness of the unhealed shame within would have reminded him that something was still lacking in who he was.

Jesus had a word for us when we recognize how little our souls can give us. You are most happy, He said, when you realize what an impoverished beggar you are in terms of things of the Spirit. "You're blessed when you're at the end of your rope. With less of you there is more of God and his rule" (Matthew 5:3, MSG). You are blessed, Jesus said, not when you recognize that you *were* poor in spirit but when you recognize that you *are* poor in spirit. Standing before God with chronically empty hands is the paradoxical open door to a fullness we can never achieve on our own.

SPREAD MY SKIRT

Another fundamental way to cover up our shame and worthlessness is to use other people. Relationships are central to spiritual and psychological health, but if we are honest, we have to admit that we have used people as surely as we have used possessions and achievements to fill up the emptiness inside. Finding someone to love us — no matter what the cost — is one of humanity's favorite ways to deal with the shame and worthlessness within.

We can use people in ways that seem socially acceptable, even polite, or we can do it unapologetically and directly. Whether it is an aging socialite who manipulates her children to meet her hunger for affection or a man who frequents porn sites on the web, people use people to make themselves feel better. We prostitute ourselves spiritually, emotionally, and physically, selling our souls to anyone who will make us feel loved and lovely. To put it in the very graphic terms God used, we spread our skirts.

Ezekiel 16, that startling passage we have already mentioned, pulls no punches as it describes how we spread our skirts. Its words are so raw that it is a difficult passage to read aloud in a public setting. This is definitely an R-rated prophetic message!

In this text, God depicts Israel as a harlot, selling her wares on the street corners, looking for any and every lover who will promise her a better deal. She is on the make for a man who will fill the lonely ache in her soul. But she is worse than a harlot; she has become an aging, ugly lover who pays gigolos to take her to bed. The tragedy of it all, beyond the sheer shamefulness of such lewdness, is that Israel has had the most faithful, beautiful husband a nation could have—the living God.

What Israel did in the marketplace of spirituality, many of us do in the marketplace of human relationships. We attempt to find lovers to fill up the emptiness we live with, the emptiness that only God can fill. With someone at our side to love us, our lives are full. We are not such bad people. The ache goes away, at least momentarily.

The stories of men who abandon faithful wives and families for a fling with a woman half their age are sickeningly familiar, but this is certainly not just a male phenomenon. I (Steve) know a young woman who says she really wants to believe and live like a Christian. But she can't get any traction in her faith.

Recently she left her second husband for a man twenty years her senior. Her second husband wanted the marriage; he was wealthy and could provide for her. But her new lover had an even higher limit on his credit cards. He also walked out on his family. No secrets hide behind the scenes to justify this young woman's actions—no physical abuse, no immorality on the part of her husband. She is simply restless, looking for someone new to take the emptiness away.

But this is already a past-tense story. The new love affair lasted only six months. Now she is living with another man. Two husbands, two lovers, and too many one-night stands in between. If the present guy leaves, or if she tires of him, she knows what to do. Dress up in her best high-fashion, provocative clothes and show up at the bars of the nicest hotels and restaurants in town. She knows the scene. She's always been able to hook up with a man there, and she's good at choosing the rich ones. The strategy may not last past fifty, but it works for now. When her brother confronted her, her response was simply, "I guess I'm just not one of those people made for long-term relationships."

Our culture has redefined sexual morality to justify what used to be called promiscuity. Serial bed partners are common. Sexual intercourse is expected early in the course of dating. Why the great stampede to tenuous relationships, sex without promise of commitment, and bitter endings? We are desperate to cover the shame of our emptiness and loneliness. If someone loves us, or at least desires us, then maybe we are okay. But attempting to heal our shame by any hookup means that in the end we only multiply our shame. We opt for relationships with people who also have gaping holes in their souls, thinking somehow they can fill ours. The serial sexuality of our culture both masks and multiplies the shame within.

The English novelist Graham Greene wrote about a love affair eclipsed by the pain of jealousy in his book *The End of the Affair*. In this story, Sarah pulled back from her affair with the writer Maurice, not because she no longer loved him but because she made a vow to the God she did not really believe in. At the time of the vow-making she thought Maurice had been killed, and she vowed to stop the affair if he turned out to be alive.

When she found Maurice alive, she felt compelled by something she could not understand to keep her promise. In the process of fulfilling her commitment, she came face-to-face with her own interior ugliness. At one point in her journal she struggled with the thought that God had no reason to love her or want her. Those thoughts took her to an assessment of herself and to the realization that she had used men as a balm for the unlovely shame within. She wrote out her thoughts directly to God:

> What do you love the most? If I believed in you, I suppose I'd believe in the immortal soul, but is that what you love? Can you really see it there under the skin? Even a God can't love something . . . he cannot see. When he looks at me, does he see something I can't see? It must be lovely if he is able to love it. That's asking me

to believe too much, that there's anything lovely in me. I want men to admire me, but that's a trick you learn at school—a movement of the eyes, a tone of voice, a touch of the hand on the shoulder or the head. If they think you admire them, they will admire you because of your good taste, and . . . you have an illusion for a moment that there's something to admire. All my life I've tried to live in that illusion—a soothing drug that allows me to forget that I'm a [b—] and a fake. But what are you supposed to love then in the [b—] and the fake? . . . Where do you see this lovely thing in me—in me, of all people? I can understand you can find it in Henry . . . He's gentle and good and patient. You can find it in Maurice who thinks he hates, and loves, loves all the time. Even his enemies. But in this [b—] and the fake where do you find anything to love?[1]

The insight and honesty of Graham Greene's story is powerful. Only when Sarah pulled out of the illegitimate affair did she begin to face the shame within—and only when she faced it did she begin to hear the faint call of the love of God. Her journey was hard, but in the end she began to experience healing of her heart's emptiness, the emptiness she had so diligently sought to fill with lovers.

DO A FEEL-GOOD GOD-THING

Jeremiah 6 tells a fascinating story about shame and cover-up. In this emotion-packed sermon, God's prophet thundered out a message about the impending destruction of Jerusalem and its inhabitants. But within the sermon is the recognition that no one is listening:

> To whom can I speak and give warning?
>> Who will listen to me?
> Their ears are closed
>> so they cannot hear.
> The word of the LORD is offensive to them;
>> they find no pleasure in it. (Jeremiah 6:10)

God's warning had become a reproach. Through Jeremiah, God explained why: The official prophets and priests of the nation had lost perspective. They had become completely immersed in a culture that promoted personal peace and pleasure as its driving passions.

> From the least to the greatest,
>> all are greedy for gain;
> prophets and priests alike,
>> all practice deceit. (verse 13)

Rather than risk their own security by speaking hard truth to their audience, God's appointed spiritual leaders watered down the warnings, disparaging Jeremiah's prophecies of judgment. In short, they reassured the people that nothing was wrong with them, that they were doing just fine. In the face of God's impending judgment, these preachers refused to deal with the true issues of the heart. The worship in the temple focused on an expensive show of religious devotion. The priests imported frankincense from southern Arabia and used anointing oil from a plant grown far away, probably in India (see Jeremiah 6:20). What they did was lavish and impressive, but their hearts were not open to the voice of God. God's indictment against these false prophets was stinging:

> They dress the wound of my people
> > as though it were not serious.
> "Peace, peace," they say,
> > when there is no peace. (verse 14)

As Jeremiah continued, he asked the people to evaluate the prophets. It wasn't just that the worship they led was focused on the externals. More significantly, they were disregarding and misrepresenting the very words of God. Their goal was to be warmly received by the people, not to bring them the hard truth that would lead to healing. Beyond that, they felt no sense of personal shame at the way they were conducting their "ministry." Through Jeremiah, God asked a piercing question:

> Are they ashamed of their loathsome conduct?
> > No, they have no shame at all;
> > they do not even know how to blush. (verse 15)

The sin of the false prophets was also the sin of the people. Like the prophets, the people of Judah had committed spiritual abominations. They were guilty of sin, but just as serious as their idolatry was the shamelessness of their response. They felt no shame. They did not know how to blush.

That absence of shame was itself an even more profound spiritual problem than their wicked deeds. The majority of priests and prophets, royalty, and common people were helping each other believe the lie that things were not that bad in Judah. They were working hard to deny the obvious, probably motivated (just like we are) by the conviction that we must salvage some sense of innate worth and goodness. But the spiritual and psychological death knell comes, not when we acknowledge shamefulness but when we *fail* to do so. When we can't blush, we can't be cured.

Showy, extravagant religious activity is often an attempt to cover our shame. King Saul did it (see 1 Samuel 15). The Pharisees of Jesus' day did it (see Matthew 23:27). The church of Laodicea did it (see Revelation 3:14-22). And we do it. We think that somehow our religious behavior and our displays of worship change who we are. We must be the good guys, and our religiosity proves it. But religious activity is an inadequate solution. The real solution to our shame is exposure, and that exposure can happen, just like it did in Jeremiah's day, when God sends us a tough message about sin and repentance, and we receive it.

It is important to ask the question — does the message of sin, neediness, spiritual poverty, and astonishing grace and mercy consistently find its way into our faith practices? Does it ever sink into our hearts, leaving us breathless with wonder? If the answer is "practically never," then maybe we need to consider whether or not we are using our religion to cover up what we don't want to face.

All of us are made out of the same clay. We are desperate to salvage and project a sense of our worth. All attempts to find a superficial healing for our sinful souls are attempts to avoid the real shame inside. We would prefer not to blush because blushing might lead to true self-examination, and who knows what we might find inside our souls.

The surprising truth is that God is aware of our maneuverings. His Word is filled with stories of people who do the same things we do to secure a superficial healing. His response is to expose their religious pretense — to pull off the fig leaves, to tear down the city, to break the cistern, and to call for blushing.

What strategies have you set up so you don't have to blush . . . so you can think you're healed, rather than taking up the difficult work of letting yourself be healed over time by God?

Has He exposed you yet? If so, how did it feel? How did you try to cover up again?

MAKE A GOD LIKE ME

Throughout the history of Israel, we see a nation that is repeatedly ensnared by the lure of idolatry. Events early in the Exodus amaze us. Left for forty days without Moses, the people grew restless. Forgetting the thunder and lightning at Sinai, the pillar of cloud and fire, the parting of the sea, the plagues and miracles of Egypt—things that you'd think would seal their faith and settle their doubts forever—the nation cried out to Aaron, "Make us a god who will go before us" (Exodus 32:1, NASB).

The resulting debacle was proverbial—God's people used their valuables to create their own god, a golden calf, around which they danced in a bacchanalian orgy that united worship and sensuality. As much as it may surprise us, the scene proves to be no more than a set for repeat performances by the nation of Israel that occur with the regularity of new James Bond movies.

Perhaps more surprising than what Israel did is our shock at her actions. Her proclivity for creating gods and goddesses that she worshipped was, in the end, symptomatic of human spirituality. Every culture has created its own gods and goddesses, its own source of truth, hope, power, and mystery. Whether they take the form of actual idols (such as the frightening figure of the Hindu goddess Kali with her long, bloody tongue, holding skulls in her hands) or white-coated scientists working in sterilized labs who promise answers to life's greatest needs, one persistent response to shame is the creation of a god who won't shame us anymore, who promises transcendence, power, and hope without ever asking us to face our moral failure. The result? We are cut off from the spiritual reality we were created to enjoy. Left with unmet longings, we seek our own meaning, adventure, intimacy, power, and transcendence.

God remains holy, just, and jealous for us. He cannot pretend that our sin is inconsequential without relinquishing that which is fundamental to His very identity, and to ours. So He shoots straight with us, pulling no punches in His denunciations of our sin.

But He is also love, passionately desiring the relationship that He envisioned from the beginning. Since that fatal choice in the garden, God has been about the business of seeking us—seeking *you*, wooing *you*, and dealing with the sin that separates you from Him. God's solution climaxed in the person of Jesus Christ at a place called Golgotha. He provided reconciliation that enables Him to be holy and just, even as He forgives us and restores us (see Romans 3:21-26).

In order for us to be reconciled, we must acknowledge our sin, our failure, our unyielding problem of shame. But the fact of the matter is that we hate doing that. Looking at that requirement, you might say, *No thank you. I'd prefer to find an answer that does not require an admission of shame and failure.* One way or another, we all think this way. So we create our own idols, and we seek in them an answer to our spiritual longing that doesn't require us to address what's wrong with us.

Humans have always been this way. Ancient polytheistic cultures filled their pantheons with beings whose deeds and characters were as dark as humanity's. The gods were capricious and vengeful. They engaged in sexual escapades that rivaled those of any human. The net effect? The worshipper did not have to deal with the dark stuff hidden inside his or her soul.

If the gods are simultaneously good and evil, then perhaps good and evil are simply two halves of the same whole. We see the evidence for this twisted thinking even today where unrestrained sex is still part of worship in many pagan religions. If the gods are like us, then sexual liaisons don't need to be rooted in a moral reality. You just do what you want to. No shame there! In fact, it is possible to connect with these gods by doing the very thing that temporarily satisfies your lusts—you can have illegitimate sex and call it a religious experience.

Swing over to the modern scientific world. Humans have created a world where there is no transcendent God at all. We are the acme of blind, amoral evolution. If there is a god, we are it. Our "father/mother" is the natural world, and we hope to find all the adventure, intimacy, meaning, and power we desire by expanding our ability to resolve all physical and material needs.

With the absence of a true God, all questions of good and evil are up for grabs. We are free to do whatever we want without shame. But we also lose hope. There is no lost paradise to regain, and we cannot expect healing for our deep spiritual pain—these things simply do not exist. We declare our love and allegiance to the material universe and to ourselves, and in the process we worship a god or a goddess like ourselves. But at least we feel no shame. This god expects nothing from us beyond our natural desires and behaviors. We hear no call to a greater reality.

The result of making a god like ourselves is that we end up worshipping ourselves. When we do, the degradation described in Romans 1:25 is inevitable: "They exchanged the truth of God for a lie, and worshiped and served created things rather than the Creator."

When humanity worships itself, shame is eliminated for the measure of reality has become simply the expression of our deeds and thoughts. We measure ourselves by ourselves, and we are free of all shame. We have achieved what seems to be an ultimate solution.

But the longings of our soul do not evaporate when the final measure of reality looks back at us from the mirror. We grope for something transcendent, for a story that means something, for soul-connecting intimacy, for real adventure. Out of one side of our mouths, we express the complete self-worship that is the fruit of the modern experiment and claim that all we long for is ourselves; out of the other side, we gasp out a longing for something more. We have become dangerously, spiritually schizophrenic.

THE QUESTION THAT REMAINS

Our schemes to heal or at least eliminate our shame without dealing with its source are not limited to the strategies we have described in this chapter or the previous one. We are poor and weak, rebels by nature. We are also born with endless creativity; instead of acknowledging our condition, we opt for alternative ways to cover or resolve shame.

Maybe you see yourself in the Pharisees' attempt to look good regardless of the rot within. Perhaps your efforts are best described by Cain's determination to build a culture that defied the judgment of God. You may be a wall-builder or convinced that another lover will give you relief from the emptiness inside. Perhaps as you have read these chapters, you have glimpsed the unique way you cover your own shame. The truth is, we all have our ways. And we resist the hard yet freeing path of admitting who we really are and turning to the mercy and love of Christ.

But no matter what path we turn to, we have a hard time silencing the question that still hovers at the edge of our souls: "Why do we still feel ashamed?" If we decide to walk toward God and seek His solution to our shame, we must acknowledge something is indeed wrong inside of us. We will have to admit to our inadequacy. We will have to admit that the longing still remains for transcendence, adventure, meaning, and intimacy. But God is on the other end of this hard path, drawing each one of us to Himself by the powerful emotion of shame.

Pause to Reflect

How have you tried to cover up or heal your shame on your own? Do any of the strategies we talked about in this chapter or the previous one sound like strategies you have used?

- Grab the Fig Leaves
- Build Me a Wall
- Cry for a Mountain
- Build My Own City

- Carve a Cistern
- Spread My Skirt
- Do a Feel-Good God-Thing
- Make a God Like Me

Perhaps you are aware of a strategy you employ to deal with your shame that we have not covered. How would you describe your strategy?

If you are like us, you probably justify what you do to deal with your shame. It is often a lot easier to see how misguided other people are than to face ourselves. Ponder for a while as honestly as you can. What do you do with your shame? How is what you do destructive? How does it take you away from God, who loves you?

Pause to Listen:
Jack's Story

I (Ralph) have known Jack for almost twenty years. During college, he sometimes came to a small group I led, but Jack was too impatient and too driven to stay with the group. At the same time, he was also a loyal man—the kind of friend who shows up really wanting to talk, even if several years have passed since the last conversation. When I called him about doing an interview, he was intrigued and ready to talk.

We started with the facts, many of them things I already knew. Successful middle-class family. Strong father who maintained a deep interest in his children. Decent high-school student and a good-enough baseball player to earn the admiration of his peers.

But he was well acquainted with shame. "Unless you are black, you can't get what it's like to be inside a black skin," he said. His abilities and successes, the affirmation he received from a healthy family—none of it was strong enough to shake his fear that the old racist propaganda might prove true. From early adolescence he lived with the constant fear that one C on his report card or one season of poor baseball stats would reveal the truth that he was basically stupid and a second-rate sports competitor because he was black.

After he broached the race issue, Jack's story came more freely. The question "What if blacks really were inferior in some fundamental way?" had troubled him when he was younger, and it still did sometimes even though everything inside of him knew it was a lie. The only defense he could come up with was to be successful in everything. He knew it didn't make sense to hang his identity on the crazy particulars of life—so many of them were out of his control—but it was hard not to, especially when those particulars were so important to him.

For example, he loved English literature and had a secret dream of becoming a writer—not the kind of dream a jock would talk about in the locker room. When he entered high school, he looked forward to eleventh grade and the English teacher who was known for the way she encouraged kids who wanted to write. Jack sat back in his chair and told me about the time he turned in his first paper to her: He'd gone home that night imagining the grade, the words of encouragement he would find across the title page when the teacher handed it back. But when she placed the paper on his desk the next day, a huge C+ was emblazoned above his name. Beneath that she had scrawled a question: "Is this your best work?"

"I remember covering the grade with my hand," Jack said. "I blushed and my head throbbed because I was so embarrassed and angry. I saw that the white girl next to me got an A. We had been in the same school for five years, and I always made better grades than her. So why did she get an A, and all I got was a C+? I figured that I got a bad grade just because the teacher didn't like the color of my skin. Or maybe I was no good as a writer because I was black. What black man had ever made it as a writer anyway? I couldn't think of any."

Later, in college, Jack was cut from the baseball team. He knew the coach had cut whites as well as blacks, but he couldn't figure it out. He was better than several of the players the coach retained. The only answer must be his color. Race was becoming an issue he couldn't escape.

Jack shifted in his chair. "I've never told this next thing to a white man," he said. "Right after I graduated from college, I was invited to a huge wedding reception at a country club. Early in the evening, one of the other guests handed me an empty glass and walked away. It only took a millisecond to understand why. I was black and must be the help. I left before the buffet dinner began. Everyone probably saw me this way."

How was he going to figure out what he was capable of if something as uncontrollable as his race kept setting the bar?

Anger and rebellion grew strong as Jack struggled to be great at something. Eventually these emotions took control of his heart and became weapons to help him deal with the burning shame inside. He was strong and unafraid to fight, so he joined the army with "an immense desire to see the world and kill somebody." Living out of anger led only to more shame—his actions confirmed the stereotype he was so desperately fighting.

He married a woman his family said was wrong for him, but he wasn't listening to anybody. Over time, the heartache of that difficult marriage brought him back into a relationship with Christ, but his growing faith only made his wife's heart harder. She left him after their third child was born. For years, those children he loved so intensely reminded him of his refusal to listen to his parents, his failure as a husband, and his inability as a father to hold his family together.

At thirty-five years old, Jack decided the only way to prove the shame wrong was to again work to always be the best. He developed a set of vows to himself in the process — things he absolutely would and would not do. Things he would live by in order to keep the shame at bay. But as our meal together ended, he shrugged his shoulders. "The shame's still there; I've given up thinking there is a way to shake it."

Jack had come up against a hard truth. Keeping vows you make to yourself is exhausting work because they never kill shame, only manage it. And it's lonely to always be on guard, to always try so hard. As we left the restaurant, Jack added one last thing: "I know I am getting angry all over again, and I don't want to go there."

Jack knows he's at a crossroads, but what if he quits fighting so hard to prove everything?

Will he find out his worst fears are true?

If you keep at it, if you are determined to fulfill the vows you make, what will you really get in the long run?

CHAPTER FIVE

The Valley of Trouble or the Door of Hope?

I (Steve) began to wrestle with shame as I entered my forties. Let me assure you that I didn't enter the wrestling match consciously or willingly; kicking and screaming I slid into it through a series of events orchestrated by another Conductor. At the time, I wasn't quite sure who He was.

One unforgettable month in 1990 focused the issues for me.

It was a beautiful week in July. Sally and I and our five children had joined her family for a vacation at the beach. We were in familiar territory. Sally and I had been vacationing at these beautiful shores every summer since we married. It was the place she had come to throughout her childhood, following the example of her mother, who had taken her lead from her mother.

You get the picture: four generations of fun, laughter, and joy. Perdido Bay represents countless fishing trips, sailing expeditions, skiing accomplishments, bonfires, and board games. But nothing prepared us for this particular night.

Because there were fourteen of us, we had taken two boats on an excursion to Pensacola Bay, a beautiful place just east of Perdido Bay. Weather that day was a little unsettled, but nothing seemed particularly serious as we stopped for a picnic at the waterside state park on the way back home. The dark clouds scuttling past to the north promised a good thunderstorm, but nothing unusual.

An hour later, as we loaded the remains of the picnic, the dogs, the nine children, and the five adults back into the boats, I felt a ripple of concern as I looked north. The storm had grown, and instead of just one we might have to dodge, two huge anvil-shaped thunderheads hung low above us. Since we were in between the two, depending on which way the front progressed, either one of them could catch us if it moved south. We needed to hurry home.

I am no meteorologist, and I don't understand what happened: How can one thunderstorm move south*west* and, at the same time, another nearby storm simultaneously move south-*east*? As we turned due north into the mouth of Perdido Bay, we were hit head-on with gale-force winds, blinding rain, and waves that were higher than the bows of our boats.

The sky blackened, and lightning tore the clouds, hitting the shore and bay. All power on shore was knocked out. Without the shoreline lights, we quickly became disoriented. Sally and I were in the larger boat, and we could barely keep in view the smaller boat and the five who were in it. We were making no headway against the wind, and we did not know where in the bay we were or which way the shore was.

Rather than promising safety, land itself became a threat—we might run aground or hit a pier hidden by the torrential rain. Shouting across the waves to the other boat, we decided to drop anchor and wait out the storm.

After more than an hour of unabated lashing by waves and wind, we realized how futile our efforts were. Repeated flashes of lightning revealed a nearby shoreline that appeared to be moving. Our anchors were not strong enough to hold against the wind, and we were being driven back out of the bay into the intercoastal waterway.

This was an even more dangerous place to be, and we tried again to make our way against the storm. As we started our engines, another flash of lightning revealed the prow of a huge barge bearing down on us, not fifty yards away. We urged our motors on with prayer, straining as if to help them do their job. We made it out of the way just as the barge plowed through the water where only minutes before we had been adrift and completely invisible in the darkness of the storm.

After another tortuous hour we finally entered the protected estuary where the boathouse awaited us. As we rounded the corner from the bay into the creek, the lights on shore flashed back on and the wind dropped to a whisper. Never had I felt such a sense of calm. We all broke into praise, amazed that we had survived the worst storm any of us had ever known.

I'd like to say that time of worship was the end of the story, but I can't. As we prayed in thanksgiving together, a dark shadow was cast in my heart. Fresh with the memory of terror, I remember looking into that night sky, wondering, "Where did you go, Father?"

In the course of one afternoon, a huge storm shook my deep-seated optimism and confidence to the core. The universe felt empty, unfriendly, and even malevolent. That storm was an exclamation point in a time of extended turmoil that made its way deep into my soul. Physical weaknesses, ministry challenges, confidence-shaking events, and currents of uncertainty in our family—these were realities that I could not deny. More importantly, I could not overcome them. These struggles were a stage for an even deeper battle in my soul, a battle that eventually uncovered a reservoir of shame.

Doubts and fears multiplied in random fashion in my soul. I reproached myself for the weakness of my faith. Irrational fears of death—a completely new experience—had robbed me of sleep and prolonged my recovery from illness and surgery. I had embarrassed myself in front of doctors. Church conflict would not yield to my earnest efforts to teach and lead. I mishandled the challenges to my authority from our long-term teenage houseguests, further undercutting myself in their eyes and in the eyes of my impressionable teenagers.

I had no doubt that I was at the center of these problems. The certainties of my faith began to fade. The strong, confident leader I had become over the years was on a respirator. I felt a deep sense of shame over the battles I was experiencing, and it began to snowball: "If I were stronger . . . if I had more faith . . . if I knew how to handle the conflict better . . ." I was desperate to cover up what I was feeling and hoped only to endure until it all "just went away."

ORCHESTRATED DARKNESS

I did not go willingly into the darkness of my soul; I was thrust there in a series of crises orchestrated by God. I hated it, but I could not avoid it. I came face-to-face with an undeniable fact: I was a shameful man. I was weak. I was inadequate. I could not keep my world or my faith intact. All platitudes designed to assuage me mocked my desire to be what I was not. All my cover-ups were stripped away. I had no choice but to accept the reality of my shamefulness.

I have said that this time was orchestrated by God. It was—if not directly, then at least by His sovereign permission. You may find this creates a very distasteful picture of God. It does, unless there is something deep within that needs to be exposed in order to be profoundly healed. Consider a few biblical examples of how God has worked in similar ways with His followers.

The most obvious example is Job. By sovereign permission, God gave Satan free reign to have at this man and strip him down to less than his spiritual Skivvies. Why? He wanted Job to learn for himself about the power, greatness, mercy, and love of God.

Just before Simon Peter's famous denial, Jesus told him something crucial. Peter had been boasting about his ability to stand with Jesus, even though all of the other disciples might flee. In response, Jesus said, "Simon, Simon, Satan has asked to sift you as wheat. But I have prayed for you . . . that your faith may not fail. And when you have turned back, strengthen your brothers" (Luke 22:31-32).

We may not like the implications, but they are not hard to see. Peter's inevitable collapse into shameful weakness was not an accident. It was God's design to force Peter to face and accept the darkness of his soul. Take some time to read the rest of Peter's story in John 21:15-19 where the resurrected Christ reinstated Peter. Then read Peter's first New Testament letter and look for clues of the deep healing from shame this proud boaster obtained through his "failure."

Finally, have you ever read the very challenging account of Jesus' conversation with a Canaanite woman? Matthew 15:21-28 tells the story: Jesus and His disciples were in the region of Tyre and Sidon, Gentile territory, when a woman approached them, crying out for healing for her demon-possessed daughter. At first Jesus ignored her, which only caused her to increase the volume of her cries. Embarrassed, the disciples begged Him to send her away. Jesus' reply, spoken loudly enough for the woman to hear, seems incredibly cold: "I was sent only to the lost sheep of Israel" (verse 24). In other words, He played a racial/cultural card that harkened back to the time when God's plan for reaching the world focused only on the Jewish race.

It gets worse. The woman again asked for help, and Jesus' reply seems unthinkable: "It is not right to take the children's bread and toss it to their dogs" (verse 26). Undeterred, the woman shot back, "Yes, Lord, but even the dogs eat the crumbs that fall from their masters' table" (verse 27).

Her interaction with Jesus, and especially her final appeal, is astonishingly *shame-embracing*. It's hard to grasp why Jesus treated her this way when He came to offer God's mercy and grace to the whole world, but He seems to be pushing her toward her shame. He demanded that she face it head-on, accept it, and walk through it, seeking nothing more than the raw, unadulterated mercy of God. That is exactly what she did, and Jesus' subsequent response was, "Woman, you have great faith! Your request is granted" (verse 28).

I wonder if Jesus did not orchestrate this conversation for people like you and me. We are so desperate to cling to any sense of worth that most of us fail to experience the depth of healing God offers—a healing of our identity-level shame. Unless we are forced—or orchestrated!—into our utter darkness, we will always try to wriggle away from the message of identity-level shame.

My experience of profound brokenness was like this. It was as if God had dropped me into a windowless room with only one door, and the key to that locked door was labeled "Face

Your Shame." During that time, God provided a powerful gift to me—two men who prayed for me: one a pastor in another church and the other a skilled counselor. Why they chose to pray for me, I still do not know. Except for talking to Sally, I was doing my best to keep my struggle hidden. But somehow they knew to pray for me.

Eventually, I "randomly" chose the counselor's name out of a list of Christian counselors in the area and called to schedule an appointment. I briefly described my battle with fear, anxiety, and doubt, fully expecting him to react with surprise to a well-known pastor struggling with such issues. His response to my query surprised and baffled me: "I would count it an unbelievable privilege to walk with you through whatever battles you are facing."

Our first appointment opened the door for me. After a couple of well-placed questions from Jim, I was face-to-face with the fact that my feelings of shame and failure were just the tip of the iceberg. Powerful childhood experiences and profound identity-level questions had never been resolved through my years of Christian ministry. Shame was everywhere in my soul.

HEALING INGREDIENTS

Others have told tales of personal brokenness and healing more effectively than I can, but let me list some key ingredients that were part of my healing.

First, readings in spiritual formation became my mainstay, teaching me to take my prayer life and personal relationship with God to a new level of honesty. I began to see that the process of being healed was just as significant as the final goal.

Second, God's Word was foundational to my healing. To borrow a phrase from Philip Yancey, I learned to meet "the Jesus I never knew" in the pages of the book of Hebrews, in the story of Jacob, and in the passions of the Psalms.

Finally, the prayers of those who embodied the truths of God's love and acceptance were critical—a wife who endured countless hours of anguish-filled struggles and never reproached me; a small group of friends who listened and loved; a counselor who became my brother, who heard my darkest memories and never turned away. In addition, there was one other mediator whose influence deserves more explanation.

In the midst of my struggle I met a professor and author whose ministry focuses on the transformation of the soul. He taught me that the key factor in spiritual transformation is the Fatherhood of God—becoming a follower of Christ means that we are adopted into the family of God. We literally become the sons and daughters of God through Jesus Christ (see Galatians 3:26–4:7). Our conversations centered on this concept. We prayed through Ephesians 3:14-21 and sought God's help in experiencing His Father-love.

Healing from my identity-level shame happened slowly, and it did not come simply by knowing a collection of facts. God became "Abba—Daddy" to me, and I began to actually believe the truth that I was a member of an eternal family whose Father is the living God.[1] In the context of this true family, I experienced the Father-love of God—it was in the Father's arms that I began to be a son, and only when I was a son did I become a man. I was led through very dark times, but those dark times eventually gave way to light.

THE VALLEY OF ACHOR

Joshua 7 records a tragic event in the life of the nation of Israel. Shortly after the miraculous victory at Jericho, Israel was defeated at Ai. In response to Joshua's anguished prayers, God revealed that the problem was sin within the camp of Israel. By casting lots, Joshua discovered that it was the sin of just one man, Achan. Achan had sought to enrich himself by secretly pillaging wealth from the ruins of Jericho, an act specifically banned by God.

Through the confrontation that followed, Joshua demanded that Achan own his actions openly before the nation. Achan confessed, acknowledging the disobedience and deception that led to national defeat. It was a time of intensifying shame—the shame of military defeat, the shame of deception, and the shame of personal greed.

Judgment was swift and complete. Achan, his entire family,

and all his cattle and possessions were stoned and burned with fire, a powerful lesson to the fledging nation as it began its conquest of the Promised Land. The place of this judgment is specifically noted in verses 25 and 26:

> Joshua said, "Why have you troubled us? The LORD will trouble you this day." And all Israel stoned them with stones; and they burned them with fire after they had stoned them with stones. They raised over him a great heap of stones that stands to this day, and the LORD turned from the fierceness of His anger. Therefore the name of that place has been called the valley of Achor ["trouble"] to this day. (NASB)

Achan had no way to hide and pretend. He was fully exposed in his shame, incapable of masking the tragic results of his rebellious and greedy heart. From then on, the valley of Achor stood as a testimony to the shame of this man.

Often life conspires to expose us. Storms and battles hit, and we are revealed as less than conquerors. Sickness and age take their toll, and we cannot hide our weakness. Systems collapse, and what felt like surety becomes quicksand. Our responses are inadequate or, worse yet, positively sinful. Our faith is small. Our insides are ugly. We find ourselves living in the valley of Achor, and before long it seems that we cannot escape and move to another more-promising place. We are stuck with a life that shouts failure and weakness, sin and shame. Are we doomed to be forever a testimony to inadequacy and failure, a statement of shame? Or are we inevitably just an "innocent" member of Achan's family, shamed by identity-shaping events and actions that we didn't choose?

THE DOOR OF HOPE

Is God's response to our shame and sin always full of judgment, stoning, and fire? The book of Hosea tells a different story. It is astonishing in its graphic depiction of God's love for Israel despite her constant rebellion. It is the story of a God who is willing to be betrayed, who is willing to bear the shame of a whorish wife. The power of the story lies in the fact that Hosea's very life is an enactment of the theme of the book. Read it and be amazed that God could keep pursuing, keep loving, keep being rejected . . . yet He never gives up on His bride.

In Hosea 2:5-13, God outlined the unfaithfulness of Israel and declared His judgment:

> [Israel] has played the harlot;
> She . . . has acted shamefully. . . .
> Therefore, behold, I will hedge up her way with thorns,
> And I will build a wall against her so that she cannot
> find her paths.
> She will pursue her lovers, but she will not overtake
> them;
> And she will seek them, but will not find them. . . .

Therefore I will take back My grain at harvest time . . .
I will also take away My wool and My flax
Given to cover her nakedness . . .
I will uncover her lewdness
In the sight of her lovers. . . .
I will destroy her vines. . . .
I will punish her for the days of the Baals. (NASB)

What would you do with a spouse who could only be kept faithful if you locked her up in the house? We can certainly understand that after years of enduring such harlotry and shaming, God finally determined to expose His people. After so much pain and rejection, who wouldn't want reality uncovered?

But exposing the shame is not the end of the message from God. He continued, "Therefore, behold, I will allure her, bring her into the wilderness and speak kindly to her. Then I will give her her vineyards from there, and the valley of Achor as a door of hope" (Hosea 2:14-15, NASB).

The valley of Achor is an everlasting memorial to shame and rebellion. God returned to the place of shame with His errant bride, and that's where He began to speak words of loving-kindness and even hope. What an amazing turnaround, a turnaround only God can bring about: The valley of Achor (which we seemingly can't avoid) becomes a door of hope . . . if we will hear the words of truth that expose our shamefulness. If we will admit who we are. If we will hear the words of grace and love that pour forth undeserved from the mouth of God.

If we will be betrothed to our heavenly Lover or sired by our heavenly Father. When we face the shame of who we really are, we enter the valley of Achor. God takes His children there so that the valley of Achor may become a door of hope.

Pause to Reflect

Are you at a place in your life where you are experiencing the weight of your shame?

As you read the story of Steve's walk through shame and the healing he has experienced and continues to experience, what stirred within your own heart?

Do you see places in your own story where facing your shame is, or could become, the door to hope?

Pause to Listen:
Ron's Story

Ron and I (Steve) have been friends since we met in the seventh grade. We haven't lived in the same town for years, but we have kept up with each other. I called him to see if he'd be willing to rehash his story and consider how shame was a part of it.

He agreed readily. *Vintage Ron,* I thought, *always ready to do his best to help.* He said he'd been aware of shame — although that wasn't the word he'd used to describe it — for as long as he could remember. His earliest memories circled around one prevailing belief: He was to blame, the one ultimately responsible for everything in his life.

Plenty of people had pointed out the illogic of his belief — his wife, the two counselors his wife pushed him to see, his pastor. I had as well. But despite all the counsel, Ron had concluded he was a failure at everything that really mattered.

Ron began by telling me about his father — a hero who survived several days afloat in the Pacific Ocean after his ship was torpedoed and then two years of hideous treatment as a prisoner of war. He came home to marching bands, flags, and banners declaring "Local Boy Does Us Proud," but his reentry into America became its own protracted battle, its own prison. What do you do after you're a "war hero"? Ron's father lived between the fantasy of past heroics and the shame of present underachievement. He drank to drown the disconnect, and Ron suffered the consequences.

I remembered from visiting his house as a boy that Ron's father had "had a problem with alcohol." Ron remembered his father's distance from him and his conviction that his father must be deeply disappointed by him. *I must not have what it takes to be a hero like my dad*, he thought.

But Ron determined to face his sense of worthlessness with the same tenacity his father had exhibited in wartime. "I never cried," Ron told me. "I don't remember ever crying. I never complained. By the time we met when I was thirteen, I was already a very hard worker, very earnest. But in high school, I had three seasons of high-school baseball without a single hit. I was terribly awkward with girls, and I had less than stellar grades. No matter how hard I tried to prove myself, I was always humiliated."

In college he joined the Navy ROTC and then entered the navy as an officer. He hoped this accomplishment would break something free in his heart. But debilitating seasickness plagued his career. Once again, the truth hammered his soul — he was no hero.

By his mid-thirties, when we no longer lived in the same town, Ron had settled into a deep, unshakable conviction that despite the repeated words of his wife, his friends, and his counselors, he was defective.

His faith hadn't undone this sense of inadequacy. We both had begun to follow Jesus Christ as teenagers, and he still believed the message that God loved him. He could even tell others clearly and objectively about that love. But Ron doubted he made God happy. He couldn't even make his father happy. He was simply a mid-grade person.

But, true to form, he never quit. "I just keep at it," he said over the phone the night we talked. "I'll keep compensating, surviving." I know he will. He's a responsible father and a Christian in full-time ministry. His peers respect his conscientious hard work. He tries to be for his family what he always longed for in his own childhood. He has gone with his wife to counselors and conferences; he has read the recommended books. He prays and studies the Bible.

But as we finished our conversation, I heard a resignation in his voice that was hard to accept. "You wanted to talk about shame, Steve? I'll tell you what I know. God forgives, but He doesn't fix my shame. My defects will always be exposed. That's my burden in life. I'll endure; that's all I can hope for. In the glory of heaven, it will all pass away."

Those are hard words to hear from a friend. Is he right? Is there no hope for deep healing of shame in this life?

CHAPTER SIX

A Journey over Time

Throughout this book we've shared the stories of people who have deeply struggled with the issue of shame. This struggle has impacted their relationship with God. Some have grown more deeply in love in Him; others, by their own admission, have struggled without any sense of relief or growth in their walk with God. The journey of facing shame and finding God's mercy and freedom is one that occurs over time, often decades.

Americans don't like things to take too long. We love speed and efficiency. But the Bible offers no quick solution to shame.

The journey through shame is a lifelong process, a dark trip through the fallenness of humanity into the bright and warm heart of God.

Some tire from this journey. Others avoid it, thinking all shame is destructive. Many are submerged in the shame that has been heaped on them by others, and it seems too painful, too cruel to face their own identity-level shame. But this is critical: *Shame is meant to lead us back to God.*

Let's take a look at one of the biblical heroes who exemplifies this.

PAUL'S LONG JOURNEY

It is easy to think of the apostle Paul as a man who really "got" grace. But if you notice the autobiographical bits of his story scattered through his letters to the church, he too experienced a lifelong journey through shame.

As a young man Paul (Saul at that time) was an earnest Pharisee. He described himself as "a Pharisee; as for zeal, persecuting the church; as for legalistic righteousness, faultless" (Philippians 3:5-6). Paul's starting point in his journey through shame was self-righteousness. He was faultless in terms of his behavior, so faultless in fact that he could participate in the stoning of the first Christian martyr—a privilege reserved only for the most blameless Pharisees.

After his conversion and at the beginning of his ministry, Paul revised his self-evaluation from a faultless, legalistic righteous person to the least of the apostles. He wrote to the

Corinthians, "For I am the least of the apostles and do not even deserve to be called an apostle, because I persecuted the church of God" (1 Corinthians 15:9).

Many of us still can't identify with Paul. It is hard to fathom the idea of apostleship, much less becoming one. Our sense of shame keeps us from dreaming that high. But others are like Paul — they see themselves as the ones selected for the top of the heap.

As Paul aged, his self-understanding continued to change. In his letter to the church at Ephesus, he stated, "I am less than the least of all God's people" (Ephesians 3:8). No longer is he the faultless, righteous Pharisee. No longer is he the least of all the apostles. He is now less than the least of all believers. In Paul's day the church was full of sinful people, just like it is today. The earliest Christians lied, deserted the faith, resisted God, divided churches, wrangled in lawsuits with other Christians, and lived immoral and even incestuous lives. Yet Paul had come to believe that he was less than the least of all these kinds of believers!

If Paul had stopped his slide down through shame at this point, we could all stay somewhat comfortable — *at least he didn't think he was better than us*, we'd say. But we're not let off the hook that easily. Toward the end of Paul's ministry, he wrote to Timothy:

Here is a trustworthy saying that deserves full acceptance: Christ Jesus came into the world to save sinners — of whom I am the worst. But for that very reason

I was shown mercy so that in me, the worst of sinners, Christ Jesus might display his unlimited patience as an example for those who would believe . . . and receive eternal life. (1 Timothy 1:15-16)

Was Paul kidding? Had he lost his memory? Was he leading a double life and now confessing to Timothy, his longtime friend? Was Paul really the *worst* of all sinners?

The Roman world in Paul's day had a full résumé, so to speak, when it came to sinning. Rulers subjugated people with an iron fist. Jesus wasn't the only person crucified. Degradation was a hallmark of religious worship and popular entertainment — orgies in temples, murder and gore in the coliseums — people killed their babies, got drunk, despised authority, mistreated their wives, blasphemed. Paul ministered to these people as he traveled throughout the Roman world. He knew them and knew their ways. So why was he "the worst of sinners"?

I don't think Paul was leading a double life — preaching the gospel by day and sinning by night. I also don't think Paul was overstating his case or altering his past. Rather I believe that Paul was continuing his lifelong journey of facing the shame of being a fallen, depraved human being — just like you and me. Recognizing and facing our shame rarely occur all at once. In Paul's case, he didn't degenerate over time; instead he gradually came to see the condition of his own soul more clearly. God was revealing the depths of his depravity in incremental stages throughout his life.

All this may seem overwhelmingly depressing, but it's not. God meets us in His infinite mercy and unlimited patience when we, with brutal honesty, face shame. The good news is we don't need to face it all at once. God wasn't bent out of shape when Paul didn't see the full extent of his shame and depravity at his conversion. The calling on our lives, just as it was on Paul's, is to stay on the path and to avoid creating our own solutions (see chapter 2) when the going gets tough. Because of his honesty, Paul came to experience God's mercy in the deepest, most hidden places of his heart. You can have the same experience. As you will see in the next story, normal, unsaintly people do all the time.

OGRES HAVE LAYERS

Steve told the story of his walk toward God's mercy and healing in the previous chapter. His experience was drawn out, but with a clear beginning—a storm opened an abyss that he fell into, and he wanted to find the way out. My (Ralph's) story is more diffused. My sense of shame has always been there, and my healing from it is slow, at times almost imperceptible. As I began working through the deeper issues of my soul, I was surprised to find so much bitterness, rage, greed, and shame. Most people pegged me as a quiet, peaceful, and thoughtful person. And I used to agree with that assessment.

Sometimes we are so unaware of the interior of our souls that we simply don't notice the garbage that has collected there over the years. There was a huge dump in my soul that I kept just out of sight. But the smell was still there, and when the wind blew just right, everyone close to me knew something was wrong. I even caught a whiff from time to time.

Over time I came to see I had buried many emotional memories. These memories included childhood abuse, an alcoholic father, and his death when I was a young teenager. Though I could remember the events, I had become numb to them. It took years for God to peel back the protective layers of numbness and bitterness, exposing the depth of the junk underlying my calm, friendly exterior. The first layer of junk was bitter self-righteousness, then rage and greed aimed at my father, who had failed me in so many ways. Next came rage and greed aimed at God, who had let it all happen. Beneath all this, of course, was shame. Through the uncovering I began to understand my soul. The key was acknowledging that my anger was not righteous indignation as I had originally thought; rather, it was an indication that I had more serious things to deal with—the deep and sinful imaginings of my heart.

When I became angry with others, instead of my usual inner dialogue about their faults, I began to pray, "Lord, I know I'm wrong; I just don't know where I'm wrong. What these people have done may be wrong, but, Lord, how in principle have I done those very same things?"

This prayer was my attempt to pull the log out of my own eye before attempting to pull a speck out of another's eye (see Matthew 7:3-5). God answered, and I discovered He was willing to help me see my logs.

A JOURNEY THROUGH SHAME

As anger and rage surfaced, I found a "me" who was capable of all the hatred, lust, greed, and rebellion that characterize the most evil among us. I found my father's sins to be mild compared to the state of my soul. I found that when I looked deeply and judged myself with the same standard I used to judge others, my self-righteousness smelled wretched. I deserved all I had imagined others deserved. I was now on my knees, humbled but not yet ready to receive the intimate mercy of God.

First I needed to overcome a real dilemma: I didn't like God. For years I had been told I didn't have to like someone to love him or her. That formula seemed to work well in the Christian circles I frequented. But did it apply to God? Could I love Him if I didn't like Him?

I hated that my dad had become an alcoholic after the war. Where was God then? Did He think losing my dad to alcohol was a good thing? I didn't like that my father was a poor role model. Was God too impotent to change my dad or the evils of war? Was this His view of wisdom? Was this His brand of justice? My heart, though humbled by the shame of my own sin, was still bitter at God, who had let all the past hurt happen.

God, in His patience and kindness, used several Scripture passages to break through to me. For decades I had viewed God as a distant schoolmaster involved in my life in order to teach me His truths. But I began to see his compassion and emotional response to the pain of my life: "In all their distress he too was distressed" (Isaiah 63:9). God is not standing by as a harsh schoolmaster; instead, He feels my pain and is deeply moved by it. I had stuffed God into a box that made Him so much less than He really was.

There was more to work through, however. The tables were turned on whether I could love God while not liking Him. I knew God loved me (as I loved Him), but I wasn't at all sure *He* liked *me*. So God guided me to the Psalms where King David said, "He brought me out into a spacious place; he rescued me because he delighted in me" (18:19). I began to get it. God does delight in me. Just as I cherish my own sons and daughters, He cherishes me. Again I was ashamed — the box I had put God into was so small and joyless.

And then a deeper problem revealed itself — one that probably plagues you, too. I believed that God was all-powerful, wise, and good, but evil seemed so illogical and detestable. Why did He allow it? Why hadn't He put Adam and Eve to death and ended the human race then and there? Can the good of life ever offset the evil and pain that began in that garden? Did God let human life continue so He could keep punishing us for our first parents' rebellion? For years I had no answers to those questions, but I finally began to look into the eyes of the bleeding, dying Jesus. Those eyes emanate the power, the wisdom, and the goodness of powerlessness.

Christ chose to embody powerlessness (as I am powerless in the face of evil) to bring me to the Father, who loves me with a jealous love. God's jealousy itself began to make sense. What would it say about my relationship with my wife, Jennifer, if I never cared what she did, where she went, who she was with? My love for Jennifer is made stronger and truer by my good jealousy for her and for our relationship. Along that same line, but with infinitely more passion, more tenderness, and more purity, God is jealous for me; the powerlessness of Christ on the cross made it possible for Him to reach out to me, a powerless, shame-filled man.

I was finally ready, open for mercy! Until I had drunk deeply of the shame of my self-righteousness, my sin, I could not drink deeply of the mercy of God. The drink of lifelong shame is humbling and humiliating, but it opened the way for me to drink life-giving mercy.

Beyond all my dreams, beyond all my power, and despite my worthlessness, I began to see that God's mercy is offered with intimacy. He invites us into His family. He delights in us as a jealous lover. God is a good, wise, powerful, and loving God who rejoices in us and extends mercy with the intimacy of family, of a lover!

THE GOOD NEWS

It sounds almost un-American and un-Christian to say people are not innately worthy of love. "We deserve to be loved! God created us in His image! It's our inalienable right!" That's what you're thinking, right?

Is that really the gospel? Jesus didn't come to heal well people. He came because humanity is systemically sick. Jesus does love us, but not because we deserve to be loved. If we got what we deserved, it truly would be "sinners in the hands of an angry God."[1] Or God would simply turn His back forever.

Adam and Eve were created in the image of God, and they

fell from that lofty position. We have inherited the fragmented, corrupted shadow of their original image. The good news of Jesus is not that we are finally going to get the unconditional love we deserve. Rather the good news is that *God still desires us*! He pursues us out of a jealous love that transcends human comprehension. He is our Almighty Lover. We can run to Him or from Him.

My journey through shame enabled me to experience God at a depth I could never have imagined. It has changed my understanding of who God is and who I am. Traveling through my soul's dump has led me to find God's mercy and an intimacy with Him who delights in me.

As counterintuitive as it may seem, the valley of shame *is* also the door of hope—the door that leads us to the heart of God, where we can experience God as the Almighty Lover of our souls. It takes a long time, but each step brings you that much closer until, finally, you begin to exchange the ashes of your shame for the beauty of God's mercy and freedom.

Pause to Reflect

Will you ask God for the strength and courage to face your identity-level shame inherited from your original parents?

Will you ask God for mercy to experience His jealous love at a deeper level?

Take time now to linger before Him.

CHAPTER SEVEN

Beauty for Ashes:
The Shame
Exchange

The Ghost made a sound something between a sob and a snarl. "I wish I'd never been born," it said. "What are we born for?"

"For infinite happiness," said the Spirit. "You can step out into it at any moment . . ."

"But, I tell you, they'll see me."

"An hour hence and you will not care. A day hence and you will laugh at it. Don't you remember on earth — there were things too hot to touch with your finger but you could drink them all right? Shame is like that. If you will accept it — if you will drink the cup to the bottom — you will find it very nourishing: but try to do anything else with it and it scalds."

"You really mean? . . ." said the Ghost, and then paused. . . .

"Yes," said the Spirit. "Come and try."

Almost . . . the Ghost . . . obeyed. Certainly it had moved: but suddenly it cried out, "No, I can't. I tell you I can't. For a moment, while you were talking, I almost thought . . . but when it comes to the point . . . You've no right to ask me to do a thing like that. It's disgusting. I should never forgive myself if I did. Never, never. And it's not fair. They ought to have warned us. I'd never have come. And now — please, please go away!"[1]

—C. S. LEWIS, *THE GREAT DIVORCE*

In this book, Lewis presented the issues we must face if we are to become people of true substance, people whose souls are ready for heaven. We see ourselves in the ghosts that inhabit Lewis's imaginary afterworld. Just like them, we resist the transforming work that God longs to do in us.

As ghost after ghost in *The Great Divorce* encounters a heavenly being, we know that our own hearts are being confronted as well. Will we let our grief be comforted? Will we part with our lusts? Will we give up our endless grumbling? And in perhaps one of the strangest encounters of all, will we drink the cup of our own shame? Is Lewis possibly right? Does draining the cup of shame open the way to infinite happiness?

We balk at the idea that embracing our shame will bring us the nourishment that leads to healing. But if Lewis spoke truth, then much of the teaching about shame is missing something fundamental. It encourages us to focus on deliverance from our heaped-on shame. But even if we are successful there, we still find ourselves wondering why we feel so empty and flawed.

If we long for freedom and joy, we have to be willing to ask if some of our shame rightfully belongs to us. If our only goal in terms of shame is recovering from the shame of what other people have done to us, then we will not see our own sinfulness. But as we gain understanding and begin to accept our sinfulness, we then come face-to-face with our need for mercy, for God to do His good work in us and for us, even though we deserve the opposite from Him.

The mercy we are offered in Jesus Christ brings forgiveness. But it is more than that; it is also an offer that transforms our very identity—we are invited into the family of God as adopted children. Christians call that identity-level change *transformation*.

I (Sally) get a sense of what transformation means when I think about houses. Steve and I have bought several old houses in our life together. The condition of the house and how much money and time we had determined the types of changes we made.

At the most basic level, we might repaint a room. We did that with our first little house in New Jersey. The next step (we did this to an old farm house in Iowa) is remodeling or adding on a room. But a category exists beyond redecorating, remodeling, or building an addition—that category involves transforming an entire house, a process that is never really "finished."

We took on such a project in Chapel Hill, North Carolina, three years ago. A house transformation means the architects, landscapers, and interior decorators join with the homeowners, the general contractor, the craftsmen, and the laborers to "remake" an existing house. When the work was finished, our house still sat on the same piece of property—we didn't tear it down and start over. It is still in the truest sense the same house. But it's a new house, a beautiful house, with all the richness and quirkiness of its past and all the goodness of things remade and working right.

Transformation is like that: You are still you, but you are also being transformed. That's why this issue of drinking the full cup of our shame is such a big deal. It's the "go-ahead" for God to begin the transformation in earnest. If we insist the old us is just fine—that it only needs a little redecorating, a small addition, or a few minor repairs—we are not admitting to the desperateness of our problem. But what does transformation into a full-fledged child in the family of God actually look like?

JACOB THE SUPPLANTER

Years ago, I (Steve) began to explore the life of Jacob. He has become a fundamental figure in my understanding and experience of spiritual transformation.

You may be familiar with his story; it begins in Genesis 25:19. Rebekah, the wife of the Jewish patriarch Isaac, was pregnant. The pregnancy was unusually stressful, and Rebekah asked God directly, "Why is this such a difficult pregnancy?" In response, God told her that she was carrying twins and that these twins would be the progenitors of two nations.

God was very specific about another crucial point. In contrast to normal expectations and inheritance laws, the older twin would serve the younger. The unborn children tumbling in her womb were evidence of a conflict that would continue throughout their lives (see Genesis 25:22-23).

When the sons were born, the second came out of the womb with his hand firmly holding the heel of the first. The firstborn, ruddy and hairy, was named Esau. The second was named Jacob, which means "supplanter." Jacob's very name creates an image of someone who manipulates his world, determined to push his way to the front of the line and get what he wants for himself. And he lived up to his name. The issues that drove Jacob were (surprise!) money, possessions, position, power, and women.

According to the custom of the day, the oldest son, Esau, was destined to inherit the majority of his father's estate. This did not mean that Jacob would be left penniless, but Esau would have the lion's share of the inheritance and the responsibilities of leadership. As firstborn son, Esau would be given the position and the financial resources to oversee and support the family's household and holdings after Isaac's death.

On the other hand, Jacob had much to anticipate as well. God had made it clear that he would eventually be in a position of leadership, even over his older brother. Rebekah undoubtedly reminded him of that promise. The precise shape of the fulfillment and how it would come about were still in the unknown future, but this family had a history of seeing God prove faithful to His promises and intervene in miraculous ways in the lives of His people. Isaac, Rebekah, and especially Jacob could rest in the confidence that God would keep His word. Jacob would have a fruitful, influential life. But this supplanter, aided by his conniving mother, was not inclined to rest in faith and wait for God to keep His promises. He took matters into his own hands.

One particular day, taking advantage of Esau's extreme hunger and his evident lack of concern about spiritual matters, Jacob offered to trade a bowl of lentil stew for the elder brother's birthright (see Genesis 25:29-34). Esau agreed, and by selling his birthright, he abdicated the power and leadership that came with being the firstborn son. Jacob suddenly had gained a strong bargaining chip to claim the leadership of his family tribe. Power, honor, and position were in his hands.

But this did not satisfy his hunger. He also wanted the financial blessings and wealth associated with being firstborn. In other words, he wanted to *jacob* (supplant) Esau on every level. In time, he and Rebekah devised an elaborate plan of deception to steal Esau's blessing of wealth and prominence from Papa Isaac.

The opportunity presented itself in an event described in Genesis 27. The old patriarch, physically blind and spiritually dull-headed through his own passion for wild game (see Genesis 25:28; 27:4), was hungry for a gourmet meal. He sent Esau out to hunt with the promise that, at the end of this special feast, he would confer his best blessing on his favorite son.

Rebekah overheard this conversation and immediately got to work. She prepared a savory stew to mimic Isaac's request and created a costume for Jacob that would fool his sightless father. Within a short time, Jacob entered Isaac's chambers with a delicious meal. However, the old man was sharply suspicious. The meal appeared too quickly. The son's voice wasn't quite right. So Isaac asked, "Are you really my son Esau?"

The deceiver insisted, "Yes, I am Esau."

Isaac gave in to the ruse and conferred his formal, irrevocable blessing of abundant wealth on Jacob instead of his intended heir.

When the truth came out, nothing could be done. Jacob had bargained for the position of honor and then manipulated himself into receiving all of the wealth and blessing normally destined for the eldest son. Notwithstanding a narrow escape from Esau's murderous anger and the necessity of a self-imposed exile under the protective wing of his uncle Laban (see Genesis 27:41-45), Jacob became a wealthy, powerful man.

One thing becomes clear as we continue the story: After

these successes, Jacob's personality and determination to secure blessings did not change. In Genesis 28, God appeared to this fugitive in the middle of a stony wasteland and delivered an almost unbelievable promise of grace and blessing:

> I am the LORD, the God of your father Abraham and the God of Isaac; the land on which you lie, I will give it to you and to your descendants.
>
> Your descendants will also be like the dust of the earth, and you will spread out to the west and to the east and to the north and to the south; and in you and in your descendants shall all the families of the earth be blessed.
>
> Behold, I am with you and will keep you wherever you go, and will bring you back to this land; for I will not leave you until I have done what I have promised you. (Genesis 28:13-15, NASB)

God had chosen Jacob to be the recipient of the covenant He originally made with Abraham. Jacob's response? As always, he was looking for a way to secure the deal, so he tried to strike a bargain with God: "*If* God will be with me and will keep me on this journey that I take, and will give me food to eat and garments to wear, and I return to my father's house in safety, then the LORD will be my God" (Genesis 28:20-21, NASB, emphasis added).

I sometimes wonder why God didn't respond to Jacob's efforts to strike a bargain with a lightning bolt to the head. But the God of grace allowed this master manipulator to continue on his way.

EXILED

Arriving at a well in the vicinity of his uncle's estate near Haran, Jacob met a young woman and fell head over heels in love. As it turned out, Rachel was his cousin, the daughter of the man he hoped would protect him from Esau. The family embraced Jacob, but as the story unfolds, we see that Uncle Laban was himself a shrewd and determined businessman who saw that this talented nephew would boost his own interests. Laban was fully a match for Jacob in the game of manipulation and deception.

Laban quickly determined to use Jacob's love for Rachel for personal gain. In response to his nephew's passionate request, Laban offered Rachel's hand in marriage in exchange for seven years of labor. Starry-eyed with love, Jacob punched that time clock and completed the task as if it were a long weekend, only to be fooled in the end.

After the wedding ceremony was completed and the marriage consummated, he woke up in the dark bridal tent and uncovered his heavily veiled wife to find not Rachel, but Leah, her less-than-attractive older sister. It was only after another seven years of hard labor that Jacob finally got his prized wife.

For the next few years, Jacob and Laban played a game of mutual embezzlement and manipulation, one topping the other in a succession of tricks. Jacob consistently got the better end of the deal, but he failed to realize that what was really happening in all this was simply the fulfillment of the promises God had given him years before at Bethel. Finally, however, Jacob crossed the line with his father-in-law and decided to escape with his earnings and his family before he lost the next round of one-upmanship. He left Haran a powerful, wealthy nomadic leader and made his way to Canaan.

WRESTLING AT MIDNIGHT

Jacob had fulfilled his quest for wealth and power; it was time to return home. However, one dark cloud loomed on the horizon—Esau. Would his brother carry out the vow he made twenty-some years before to kill him on sight?

Genesis 32 reveals Jacob's fearful anticipation in the face of this potential threat. On the edge of the Promised Land, he spent a night alone, thinking and planning his entry into the homeland of his estranged brother. In the middle of the night, a stranger approached and began to wrestle with Jacob. We can only imagine what was going through the mind of the patriarch as he pushed, pulled, and sweat his way through an all-night battle with a silent, unknown foe. Did he think it was a hit man from Esau? A desert pirate? Whatever opinion we have of Jacob, it is impressive that even as a middle-aged man he had the stamina to last the night in a pitched hand-to-hand battle!

Seeing the spreading dawn, the stranger determined to end the match quickly. He touched Jacob's hip, dislocating it severely. The Hebrew word translated *touched* in Genesis 32:25

literally means "touched." A finger placed against Jacob's hip blew the joint out. It became clear to Jacob that his opponent had been toying with him the way a cat toys with a mouse. In a flash, Jacob knew several facts: This man could have ended the match at will; this was no desert pirate or hired gun from Esau; and, most importantly, this must be a supernatural being.

His automatic response is fascinating. Always seeking to expand his portfolio of blessings, Jacob grabbed this being and refused to let go. He clung like a barnacle to a pier, like a rock climber to a lifesaving handhold, and said, "I will not let you go unless you bless me" (verse 26).

The angel asked a very unusual question in response to Jacob's demand: "What is your name?" (verse 27).

We cannot escape the irony. The last time Jacob held onto a powerful man (or was held by him) was forty-plus years earlier in his father's bedchamber.

His father asked, "Who are you?"

Jacob lied, "I am Esau."

Now again he was clinging to a potential source of great blessing, and the question came once more: "Who are you?"

Jacob answered, "I am Jacob."

TRANSFORMED IDENTITY

We have seen that Jacob is the kind of guy who had power and success but very few friends. His home was a place of contention and conflict, of rivalries spawned by determination to get the wife of his choice and to gain as much wealth as possible. It is not hard to imagine the hard-bitten loneliness of this man, the shame his very name reminded him of every time he heard it.

But God is relentless with His children. He is determined for us to walk through the door of identity-level shame into a place of true healing. Salvation works its way into our souls only when we admit who we really are. We must admit we are helpless to save ourselves, to receive the gift of Christ's righteousness. Of course, it doesn't end there. Throughout life we must increasingly face our weakness and failure to be delivered by God from ourselves. We must be broken in order to experience profound healing.

At some point, to know that healing, Jacob had to own his name: "I am Jacob. I am the supplanter, the manipulator, the grasper and grabber of everything I can find. I can pretend no longer." The brook of Jabbok became the place where the early light of dawn shone on a man who, finally broken and unable to rescue himself, brought his true identity into the light of the presence of God. He owned his identity-level shame springing from character traits evident within him from conception. Only then could his name be changed by the One who has the power to transform our identity: "Your name shall no longer be Jacob, but Israel; for you have striven with God and with men and have prevailed" (Genesis 32:28, NASB).

Jacob finally drank the cup of his shame. And it turns out that C. S. Lewis was right—to be delivered from our phantom existence, we must drink from the disgusting cup. We must quit blaming others, pretending, running, sewing fig leaves, carving cisterns. We must lay aside our countless ruses by which we deny the reality of our identity. We must admit who we really are.

It goes against all friendly advice, all psychology, and most Christian teaching on the subject, but in the end the way to deepest happiness is through honest shame.

JESUS AND OUR IDENTITY-LEVEL SHAME

In current Christian understanding, many of us are able to receive the debt/guilt/payment message. The old chorus "He Paid a Debt He Did Not Owe" says it accurately, "He paid a debt He did not owe, I owed a debt I could not pay; I needed someone to wash my sins away."

We have sinned and incurred a debt that we cannot possibly pay. Just like the unjust steward in Matthew 18:21-35, we face a debt so large that we have as much hope repaying it as we would tackling the U.S. national debt. The amount of our indebtedness is outlandish and hopeless. God's response is "I forgive it—all of it—because my Son has paid the full price. All of the demands of My justice have been satisfied through the infinite provision of the death of the Son of God" (see Romans 3:21-26).

Can it be that shame is handled the same way as our indebtedness? Can it be that just as Jesus Christ paid the actual debt, He also bore the actual shame of our identity at birth as abandoned children, thrown onto the garbage dump, swimming in blood, and deserving death (see Ezekiel 16)? Can it be that He bore the shame of our identity as Canaanite dogs (see Matthew 15) or as master manipulators and deceivers like Jacob (see Genesis 27)?

The cross of Jesus is not just about forensic guilt and an impossible debt. It is also about identity-level shame that is exposed for the world to see and to mock. Jesus was jeered by the masses in Jerusalem. He was ridiculed by the Pharisees, mocked as a helpless liar. He was crucified, naked and exposed—an unimaginable shame for a Jewish man. A laughingstock, He was spat upon, abused, and victimized—think of what this felt like! All of the shameful treatment and exposure you might feel in your soul was heaped on Him in one outpouring of vitriolic hate.

It is not just about what happened *to* Jesus; it is about what happened *in* Him. The anchor of His soul had always been His Father's love and care, but on the cross, He experienced abandonment and rejection. That total loneliness is heard in His agonizing cry, "My God, My God, why have you forsaken me?" (Matthew 27:46). It's not just about guilt; it is about the shame of abandonment, experiencing life with no center or hope in God. Jesus had always been strong and immovable. Now He was silent. He did not rebuke His accusers. He took the role of littleness, of weakness, of brokenness and death.

Peter described the cross as an experience of shame (see 1 Peter 2:21-24). According to the author of Hebrews, by embracing the cross Jesus "despised the shame" (12:2, NASB). But perhaps the most powerful image comes from the prophet Isaiah:

> The Lord God has given Me the tongue of disciples,
> That I may know how to sustain the weary one with
> a word.

He awakens Me morning by morning,
He awakens My ear to listen as a disciple.
The Lord GOD has opened My ear;
And I was not disobedient
Nor did I turn back.
I gave My back to those who strike Me,
And My cheeks to those who pluck out the beard;
I did not cover My face from humiliation and spitting.
For the Lord GOD helps Me,
Therefore, I am not disgraced;
Therefore, I have set My face like flint,
And I know that I will not be ashamed. (50:4-7, NASB)

According to Isaiah, Jesus has been entrusted with the ministry of speaking words of sustaining power to the weary—the living words of God. In part, this ministry comes to Him because He Himself is the supreme example of one who listens, receives, trusts, and obeys the Word of God. He can show us how to listen to God. He is the perfect example of a true disciple.

But even more than giving us an example to follow, Jesus' ministry also gives life to us because He received life through total, radical obedience to the Father. He was sustained by the word of the Father, and He depended on the Father in exactly the same way that we are called to. In His obedience and dependence, even to embracing the shame of the cross, Jesus Christ experienced the power of God.

THE SHAME OF THE CROSS

At some point it became clear to Jesus that the Father's will included the most shameful experiences a man can face — total exposure, full rejection, complete abandonment, helplessness, mockery, and accusation. His closest companions misunderstood Him. The crowd believed the worst about Him. He was silent before the heaped-on shame. His hands hung limply at His side, unable to wipe away the spit trickling into His eyes. They jerked at His beard until it was ragged and bloody. Everyone saw His friends desert Him. His clothes were stripped away as His body was nailed to the cross. He lost the ability to control bodily functions. And finally the Father turned His back on Him as He bore the sin of all humanity.

As strange as it sounds, Jesus became sin for us on the cross (see 2 Corinthians 5:20-21). Why? Jesus exchanged all that He was for all that we are — our sin, our guilt, our debt, our curse, and our shame. This is not just some spiritual hocus-pocus. He actually bore it all and became it all. He took and became all the shame you feel and all the shame you bear so you wouldn't have to bear it, or be it, anymore.

Shame. Jesus Christ embraced it. It was the Father's plan. Why? The answer is remarkably simple: He wanted sons and daughters, a family to love and be loved by. Just as we need His righteousness in exchange for our guilt, we must have our shame exchanged for His Sonship, our ashes for His beauty, our weakness for His strength. Take a moment to slowly go through the questions below and allow God to whisper in your ear as you sift through the ashes of your shame.

Pause to Reflect

Sit with the truth that Jesus has fully taken your shame as well as your guilt upon Himself. What is it like to see your shame on Jesus?

Are you aware of places in your life, your heart, your memories that are indeed ashes?

What beauty do you long for?

How does your heart respond to God's offer of beauty?

Do you see places in your story where God is indeed exchanging beauty for ashes? Journal about where you see this exchange taking place.

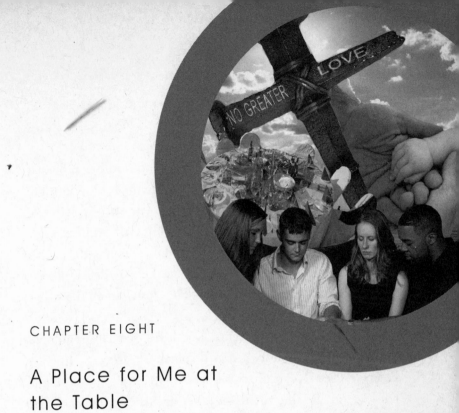

CHAPTER EIGHT

A Place for Me at the Table

Our hope is that by now you are more hopeful that your identity-level shame can be deeply and substantially replaced. We have told parts of our own stories so that you could see how the love of God is reshaping our souls. Remember Frances, the young African American woman who now directs a crisis pregnancy center? She's a real person, and her healing is real and still growing. Be encouraged!

We've examined how the Scriptures speak to the issues of our shame. Jacob was finally able to say, "My name is

Jacob, the supplanter, the grabber, the manipulator"; and in that confession he found what he had been looking for all his life—the blessing of God.

We've also looked at the salvation that God has provided us in Jesus Christ through the biblical lens of adoption. He has done much more than just pay for our sin through the cross. He has taken our shame upon Himself and born the ugliness. Beyond that, God has invited us to come home with Him. He delights in being our Father. He has declared that we will share equally with His first Son, Jesus, in all the riches He has for us.

As unbelievable as it seems, God loves us even though He knows full well what we are made of. In *The Message*, Eugene Peterson tried to capture this liberating reality: "But God put his love on the line for us by offering his Son in sacrificial death while we were of no use whatever to him" (Romans 5:8). Jesus, the Son, is in full agreement with His Father's desire to make us part of their family. This One who is our brother, this One who has agreed to a revolutionary redistribution of the wealth of heaven, is delighted to share what is rightfully His. More than that, He feels a deep affection for us. The writer of Hebrews made the startling claim that Jesus Christ is not ashamed to call us His brothers (see Hebrews 2:11).

And yet . . . and yet . . . our shame can be stubborn. It is like black mold growing in the basement of our souls. It's not enough to bleach the walls or use a mold-killing paint. The damp source that feeds the growth of the mold has to be cut off. Sometimes part of the structure itself has to be replaced. Studs or wallboard or flooring has to be ripped out. Like mold, shame spreads, causing ever greater damage. Like mold, it is unlovely, debilitating, and even toxic. So how do you learn to walk through your own shame and find the love of God in the midst of it?

As we shared at the beginning of the book, the four of us discovered that academic and theological understanding does not heal the shame within our hearts. We spent a lot of time discussing the nature of shame, the biblical truths about it, the ways we try to manage it, and even the stories of other people's struggles with shame. But simply talking about this stuff left our own souls virtually untouched. Our shame, the heaped-on kind as well as identity-level shame, is more deeply healed through pursuit of true Christian community.

We had to talk about our lives with one another, letting ourselves be known; through this process *we found ourselves still loved*. The reality of God's love has to be experienced through the faithful love of people who truly know us. This is not a new truth, but it's one that we reaffirm and place before you: True Christian community is God's designed healing place for shame.

The sad truth of the matter is that this depth of community is little known to most Christians. And even though we strongly encourage you to pursue and develop such community, this is not a how-to book on developing profound, lifelong friendships. For now, we can only urge you to pursue that goal by:

- Prayerfully and diligently seeking to strengthen your friendships so that love, acceptance, and forgiveness abound. If you already know that kind of spiritual family, you are profoundly blessed. If you do not have it, seek it diligently. Sift through your relationships until you find that one friend, that one couple, who wants to go to a deeper heart level. Risk exposing your true self to that person. Be willing to receive another person without judging him or her.
- Find a book that calls for true Christian community (*Community and Growth* by Jean Vanier or *Life Together* by Dietrich Bonhoeffer are two helpful books about building real relationships), read it with someone, discuss it, and pray about the principles and practices it teaches. Practice what you learn.
- Don't wait to be asked. Invite someone to go for coffee, for lunch, for a walk. Open up about your fears and questions — not as counselors seeking to answer each other's questions but as friends whose great gifts include listening hearts, honest wrestling with truth, and faithful, persistent love.

While you're seeking and praying for that kind of healing community, there is plenty you can do on your own. Nothing should hold you back from beginning the journey through the darkness of your soul. All you need to begin is what you already know about your heart. Remember that the journey to know yourself better is also the journey to know God. John Calvin expressed that hope when he wrote: "Every person, therefore, on coming to the knowledge of himself, is not only urged to seek God, but is also led as by the hand to find him."[1] And as you find Him, your most profound experience of healing will happen in the heart of God's love, the family of the Father, the Son, and the Spirit.

We want to give you some practical help as you begin to walk through your shame to the abundant love of God. This chapter is a series of experiences to open up the vista of that love to you. You can begin (and return) to these formational exercises as God takes you further and further along. You can also use these exercises to build a community by sharing them with another person. Our prayer is that the conversations sparked by this book and these exercises will help you experience the healing mercy of God.

PAUSE TO RECEIVE: BELOVED OF GOD

Adoption isn't just a metaphor for salvation; it's reality. One of the great truths of Scripture is that God doesn't just invite us to believe something—He invites us to belong to Him. Eugene Peterson's paraphrase of 2 Peter 1:17 says, "This is my Son, marked by my love, focus of all my delight" (MSG). The truth is, every Christ follower is loved in the same way by the Father: "You are my son or daughter, marked by my love, focus of all my delight." The apostle Paul spoke that same reality to us: "For you did not receive a spirit that makes you a slave again to fear, but you received the Spirit of sonship. And by him we cry,

'Abba, Father.' The Spirit himself testifies with our spirit that we are God's children" (Romans 8:15-16). The apostle John said it as well: "How great is the love the Father has lavished on us, that we should be called children of God! And that is what we are!" (1 John 3:1).

But what does this adoption actually mean in real life? To find out, Sally called a couple who had adopted four foreign children when their one biological son was fourteen years old. These children, all girls, had been raised in extreme poverty in a preindustrial, chaotic environment. The health, nutritional, and educational standards so essential in caring for children had only been minimally addressed. Furthermore, these girls had never experienced simple things that are part of everyday life in the West—cars, telephones, electricity, or running water.

But the loss these girls suffered went far deeper than inexperience with modern tools. They had been utterly neglected. Because of their harsh circumstances and distress in their own souls, the girls' parents had not provided for their most basic needs—food, physical touch, baths, clean diapers, clean clothes, tenderness. Their mode of instruction was anger and verbal shaming. When the oldest of these girls was only nine, all four sisters were put in an orphanage. Compared to the home they shared with their alcoholic parents, the orphanage represented a decided improvement, but it could never be described as a home.

Unfortunately, life is not like the musical *Annie*. Being whisked to a new environment doesn't change everything. The adopting mother told us that when they brought these girls into their home, they had to teach them to hug and to kiss. They had to teach them to look their new parents in the face. Their shame was so thick they could not bear the vulnerability involved in seeing and being seen by another person, even a person who had clearly declared she wanted to love them for the rest of their lives. As this mother put it, these children she deeply wanted and had chosen still struggled with a core feeling of unworthiness.

The girls moved from an orphanage to a beautiful home, from parents who had neglected them at the most fundamental level to parents who included and loved them. They received medical care, new clothes, toys, beds of their own, good family meals, quality education, special times of holidays and vacations and family events. But still the doubts lingered: "I am different. There is something wrong with me that isn't wrong with the people around me."

The parallel between these girls' experience and the experience of many Christians is striking. A person can put his trust in Christ, know he has been made a part of God's family, enjoy many of the benefits of a cleaned-up, better life, and still struggle at a deep interior level.

These wise parents understood their mission. They knew the answer wasn't just to provide for the girls' physical needs or to teach them all they needed to know to be successful adults in their new country. They understood that their daughters needed two things most of all. First, they needed constant reassurance that they were loved unconditionally, forever. So they declared again and again, by words and actions, that they would never withdraw their love. They would endure everything. They dealt with wrong behaviors, but they maintained their love. They spent hours holding one of the little girls who especially needed physical closeness for reassurance. They comforted their daughters again and again with the truth—they would never turn them out, never give up on them. They would be family forever.

Second, they needed to know that their adoption was part of a greater story. "God has placed you in our family," they would tell their daughters again and again. "He is working out a story for your lives within the greater story of His love." The goal was to help the girls understand that all of the parts of their lives—the dark as well as the bright—were essential to the design of their true Father for them, *His* daughters.

Of course, each daughter is different. Their healing is happening at different rates and in different ways. One needs to grieve the rejection she feels from her biological parents more deeply than the rest. Another needs more discipline, instruction, and forgiveness for wrong habits that are hard to break.

These girls were fortunate to be adopted into a family that already had an older brother. He is convinced, along with his parents, that adopting these new sisters is exactly the course God intended for his family's life. And he is aware of the financial implications of his family's decision. He understands that their choice means that he has forfeited most of what would have been his inheritance. The adoptions were costly, and one day what would have been only "his" will be divided five ways.

Knowing that, he still has embraced his new sisters as eagerly as his parents have.

NOW IT'S YOUR TURN . . .

Picture your own story as a story of adoption. Listen first to what Paul said in Ephesians 2:13,19:

> Now because of Christ—dying that death, shedding that blood—you who were once out of it altogether are in on everything. . . . That's plain enough, isn't it? You're no longer wandering exiles. . . . You're no longer strangers or outsiders. You *belong* here, with as much right to the name Christian as anyone. God is building a home. He's using us all—irrespective of how we got here—in what He is building. (MSG)

Next, ponder some of the implications from the adoption story you just read. Like these sisters, have you experienced neglect and poverty in your own life and soul? In what ways?

Perhaps you believe the gospel in every way you know how, but at the same time you still operate with a deep sense of unworthiness. If you do, imagine being a child in this family we just talked about. Imagine a wise and patient mother and father holding you, talking to you, promising you again and again that they will never leave you. Let those words bathe your heart and mind. Feel their arms around you. These parents know the ugliness you feel, the ugliness of what is in you, but you are still their little child. They delight in you.

Now ponder this question: "What if God is really like that?"

Imagine the Spirit of God teaching you to call God your "Abba Daddy." Can you call Him that now, out loud?

Imagine your big brother, Jesus. He is like the big brother in this true story. He, too, is convinced that you are meant to be part of God's family. He, too, gave up sole rights to His inheritance in order to bring you into the family. He is not ashamed of you, and one day He will share all God gives Him with you (see Romans 8:16-17). Think about how you would feel if you were welcomed into a family by a big brother who chose to open the door for your adoption, knowing full well that it would cost him nearly everything. Will you let yourself be loved by a big brother like that?

PAUSE TO RECEIVE: THE WELCOME WE ARE AFRAID TO TAKE

George Herbert lived only forty years, from 1593 to 1633. He was the fifth son of a prominent family, and his mother was devout, intelligent, and highly involved in the political and intellectual circles of upper-class England. Herbert became a Latin scholar at Cambridge University and then went on to become the public orator of the university, the chief formal spokesman for the school. His goal was to become involved in political life. At first all went well. He had the favor of King James I and two influential patrons. But over the course of several years, James I and the patrons died. The new king, Charles

I, showed little interest in Herbert.

So, at thirty-seven Herbert left London and became an Anglican priest. He had married only the year before that. His pastoral ministry was in an obscure small town. As you might imagine, his life was marked by a very profound sense of disappointment and failure. He didn't live up to his pedigree; his first-choice career was crushed; and he ended his short life in a tucked-away corner of the country.[2]

Although his biography contains no great debaucheries or searing tragedies, Herbert experienced his own shame and wrestled deeply with the love of God in response to his disappointments. But even though he struggled honestly, it seems he never really comprehended the story that God was writing through his life. He could not see the profound way he was being touched and changed by God.

None of us really do, though. Part of an authentic Christian journey is that what we often feel about ourselves and our progress is only the poverty of our heart. We do not feel what we think we should as Christians and children of God. We believe that we have not changed or made a contribution to God's work the way we should.

George Herbert would understand. He wrote what many consider to be one of the finest collections of religious poetry in the English language, yet none of his work was published in his lifetime. He did not even share his poetry with his friends. In fact, it was only on his deathbed that he sent copies of his work to his friend Nicholas Ferrar. Attached to the poems was a note saying that if Ferrar thought the poetry might help any "dejected poor soul," he was free to publish it. If not, Ferrar was instructed to burn his friend's work. We can be grateful that Ferrar understood the value of what Herbert entrusted to him.

Now, almost four hundred years later, Herbert's poetry can help us understand our souls. He was a man determined to know the love of God, but he was also like the rest of us—a person whose understanding of that love ebbed and flowed. He knew the world of doubt and shame. Listen to the conversation between doubt and confidence in this poem:

Love (III)

Love bade me welcome, yet my soul drew back,
  Guilty of dust and sin.
But quick-eyed Love, observing me grow slack
  From my first entrance in,
Drew nearer to me, sweetly questioning
  If I lacked anything.

"A Guest," I answered, "worthy to be here";
  Love said, "You shall be he."
"I, the unkind, the ungrateful? ah my dear,
  I cannot look on thee."
Love took my hand and smiling did reply,
  "Who made the eyes but I?"

"Truth, Lord, but I have marred them: let my shame
  Go where it doth deserve."
"And know you not," says Love, "who bore the blame?"
  "My dear, then I will serve."
"You must sit down," says Love, "and taste my meat."
  So I did sit and eat.[3]

NOW IT'S YOUR TURN . . .

What objections did Herbert offer to Love's invitations? What did Love say to override those objections?

Very often, we are like Herbert. Even if we do respond to the invitation, we are determined that we will somehow pay our own way (or at least part of it). We will not be freeloaders. We will not mooch.

Look up the story in Matthew 18:21–35. A slave owed the king ten thousand talents. Although the actual value of a talent at the time of Christ is not known, many scholars think each talent represented the total of a fifteen-year wage. Let's call that wage $12,000 a year, or $180,000 per talent. Ten thousand talents would then equal $1.8 billion. It's an unthinkable amount, an impossible debt to clear before you die.

Look at the slave's statement in verse 26. He was going to attempt to repay his entire debt! Or at least that was his claim. Do you think he really heard the master's reply in verse 27, releasing him and forgiving the debt? Why didn't he "get" it?

Jesus told this story to show how God's forgiveness of us is meant to breed our forgiveness of others. But it is also a good story to help us realize how much forgiveness God has to offer through Christ. The Greek word for "forgive" or "cancel the debt" in this story is the same word used in 1 John 2:12: "I write to you, dear children, because your sins have been forgiven on account of his name." You may feel you are too far gone to be forgiven, but it's not true. God always has more forgiveness than you have sin. That's the reality of the gospel.

Think about your life through the lens of this parable and Herbert's poem. Do you see ways you are trying to pay God back? To work off your debt? In the poem, Love does not deny the objections Herbert makes, but Love still makes an offer. What is Love's offer? What does Love most want in this poem? Committed workers? Faithful servants? Obedient followers? Or something else?

Now read Revelation 19 and think about the culmination of humanity's story as it is revealed in that chapter. What awaits those of us who believe in Christ? A judgment hall? An awards banquet? Or a wedding with us as the bride?

You are forgiven. No matter how dark your heart looks to you, how sickening your choices may have been, God has paid for it all by Christ's death on the cross. As the apostle John came to understand, "We will know by this that we are of the truth, and will assure our heart before Him in whatever our heart condemns us; for God is greater than our heart and knows all things" (1 John 3:19-20, NASB).

You are invited to Love's table. Will you let go of all your objections and just sit and eat?

PAUSE TO RECEIVE: WHOSE SIDE OF THE LEDGER?

Throughout this book we have talked about two different kinds of shame: heaped-on shame and identity-level shame. Our fear is that you would hear us saying, "Every bit of shame you feel, you deserve to feel." That's not true at all.

Shame has two very distinct sources even though they often merge and twine around each other so that we have a hard time separating them. The shame described in the stories in chapter 2 is heaped-on shame. That means we don't deserve it; it's not really about us even though we may struggle with the excruciating feeling that we deserve every bit of it.

Heaped-on shame can be devastating. Sexual and verbal abuse lash the unprotected. Racial prejudice is an inherited legacy—there is nothing you can do about the way you were born. Physical deformities often cannot be corrected. The shame of being deserted by your adulterous spouse or by your father or mother stings for a lifetime. Never really succeeding in a career makes you want to hide. Your inability to find a spouse or have children can feel like it is being broadcast on every channel.

Ultimately, shame like this does not arise in our hearts because we are worthless people. It is heaped on us. We live in a deeply flawed world populated with people and circumstances that damage us. They evaluate us wrongly. They do things to us that wound and destroy. Many of these arrows enter our souls long before we can defend ourselves, and we believe the lies. Then we conclude that we are magnets attracting shame because we are worse than anyone else. The challenge is that heaped-on shame catalyzes true identity-level shame. Remember Frances, the woman who said that if people think you are trash, you might as well do trashy things?

As we said in chapter 3, identity-level shame does have its root in our souls. We were born in sin. We are guilty before God, and that true shame must be walked toward. Remember the quote from C. S. Lewis? The Spirit told the Ghost that she needed to drink the whole cup of shame. As unbelievable as it sounded, she would find it nourishing. The shame that is really ours must be owned and embraced. As we accept our shame, we will find the mercy of God. On the other hand, the shame that has been heaped upon us needs to be named for what it is and rejected.

It is good to spend time learning to distinguish between real identity-level shame and heaped-on shame. Although life can never be simplified and totally bisected into a column of what belongs to me (that is, my real shame) and a column of the shame that has been wrongly put upon me, it is still good to grow in our ability to discern between these two sources of shame.

You might want to take this opportunity to do just that. Take a sheet of paper; draw a line down the middle. Label one side "heaped-on shame." Label the other "my real identity-level shame." As you think back through issues in your life, decide which column they best belong in. Don't stop to analyze or to feel bad that you feel bad about something. Just write it all down.

When you think you are finished, take a look at the list

under "heaped-on shame." Begin to speak the truth of God to these issues. Read the Bible in earnest, asking God to give you answers for the lies you have believed. As you find God's answers to the lies of your heaped-on shame, write those truths out.

A young woman I (Sally) was talking to just this week fastened a stack of three-by-five index cards together on a metal ring. On those cards she wrote the lies she had believed about herself, and then on the other side, an answer from Scripture that refuted that lie and helped her know what to believe instead. She has carried around that little binder of cards for more than a year, and the truth is setting her heart free.

You may prefer a different methodology. Perhaps you need to tell your story to a counselor or a wise friend, or to seek out someone who can pray with you in a way that brings healing. The point is, we need a bigger reality than our own self-encouragement to break free from heaped-on shame.

Now to the second column. Identity-level shame is tougher to face. For many of us, it is hard to make a list of all the ugliness we see inside. How does a person keep from drowning in it? The following Scripture passages may help direct your heart toward the love of God so He can speak His love into the real shame you bear.

Not "A" but "The": Luke 18:9-14 (NASB). Do you see what the tax collector in this story called himself? Not "a" sinner, but "the" sinner. What is the difference between these two words? What is the point the tax collector made?

What is the solution? Why did Jesus tell this story? He said it's not about how hard we try or how well we do (the Pharisee in the story was obsessed with his own effort and successes), but about how honestly we turn to God's mercy.

What does *mercy* mean to you? Explore this word. Use your dictionary, a biblical concordance, and your imagination.

Stay Long Enough to Hear the Love: John 8:1-11. In your imagination, take your place in the crowd gathering around Jesus in the story that begins in John 8:1. Everyone in this story is going to be shamed by Jesus, but only one remains long enough to learn what it means to walk through shame to forgiveness and healing. Look at what Jesus said to this woman. What would it mean to take her place in the story and learn true freedom?

Take your place beside this woman. Listen to Jesus speak His truth to you. Do you hear His offer of healing?

Healing Is a Gift, Not a Wage: Isaiah 53:5. Isaiah 53:5 makes a promise: "[Jesus] was pierced through for our transgressions, He was crushed for our iniquities; the chastening for our well-being fell upon Him, and by His scourging we are healed" (NASB).

1 Peter 2:24 reassures us of this same reality: "He Himself bore our sins in His body on the cross, so that we might die to sin and live to righteousness; for by His wounds you were healed" (NASB).

Go back to the column on your chart that speaks of your real identity-level shame. Jesus' death is able to heal your soul. What an incredible concept—soul healing! What wounds do you bear in your soul that need profound healing? Describe the darkness that you see and feel within. Reflect on the things you are most ashamed of about yourself, the things you hate most. Understand that Jesus Christ desires to heal you in these places.

Healing is a gift, not a wage. Ponder the implications of that statement. What does it mean about the giver of healing? What does it mean about the receiver of healing? Why do you think deep healing has been an elusive experience for you?

We need a more profound healing than simply learning to think correctly. Correct thinking is essential (see Romans 12:1-2); at the same time we cannot think our way out of our shame. We need to be touched in ways beyond the scope of our intellect.

Will you simply begin to pray healing for yourself? Will you ask someone you trust and respect to begin to pray for you?

PAUSE TO RECEIVE: THE ONE WHO ALREADY KNOWS

As a teenager, long before I (Sally) understood shame intellectually, I lived with its presence in my life. At some point in my teen years I wrote a poem to try to explain what I felt to God. It was bad poetry, and thankfully the poem has been lost. But I do remember the first line: *I don't apologize for what I am / My shame is deeper because I know / that you already know.* Somehow at age sixteen, with a very loving upbringing where I had not done anything drastically sinful or wrong, I still understood that inside I was an unlovely and truly sinful person.

What really got to me was my awareness that God must have known that truth long before I knew it. Yet He had chosen to love me and even die for me without having to point out how deeply flawed I was. That was an acutely embarrassing realization. Like having dinner with new friends and being told after the fact that you had spinach in your teeth from the first-course salad, it's just shameful. If we're with friends when this happens, we say to them, "Why didn't you tell me? It's so much better to know and do something about it."

But as I thought about God Almighty, I realized He couldn't "just tell me," at least not all of it, all at once. My sin is so immense, my fallenness so fallen from His holiness, that if I could see what I really am, my reaction would be like Isaiah's when he saw the Lord. He fell on his face and said "Woe is me; I'm a dead man." It took an angel to revive him and a burning coal to cleanse his lips (see Isaiah 6:1-7).

So God in His mercy doesn't let me see all of me at once. When I began to realize He had been loving me all along, overlooking so much, the first thing I felt was shame. But now as an adult, as I sit with that shame, healing and relief begin to grow. If He already knew and loved me, maybe He really is with me, forever. He can't discover anything that will send Him away because He already knows it all. My only choice is to *fall into* that sort of love or to pull back from it and declare that I only want to be loved when I have earned it. One is a choice through shame to life; the other is to embrace spiritual sterility and death.

NOW IT'S YOUR TURN . . .

I don't know how my poem ended. But each one of us has to decide. What will we do with the God who already knows? It might be good to take a look at Hagar's story in Genesis 16. She was both victim and victimizer. Her first discovery was that the God who saw all chose to spare her life. In her second encounter with Him, found in Genesis 21:1-21, she discovered that in the midst of complete rejection by the only family she knew, God stayed with her and provided for her. Read her story in both chapters and think about the God who sees and knows you and still stays near.

Why don't you make an attempt to finish my poem?

I don't apologize for what I am
My shame is deeper because I know
That you already know . . .

PAUSE TO RECEIVE: SHAME ON BOTH SIDES

It's an interesting reality that when a family member, especially a spouse, does something shameful, the person who feels the most shame may not be the perpetrator but the offended party. We (Steve and Sally) have a friend whose husband left her, their three children, and the ministry for another woman. His actions were blatant and public, played out before a large church. This man rejected counsel, support, love, and faithful discipline from dozens of highly committed friends and relatives to make his leap into self-fulfillment. Years later his children are still reeling from the confusion and abandonment.

Yet the rest of the story is so commonplace that you could fill in the details. It is not the man who exhibits any shame—he is tough, hard, and arrogant. It is his wife. More than a decade later she still has a hard time going to church. She is just beginning to relate openly to old friends. Granted, this tragedy has brought some deep issues to the surface, and God is at work in her life. Still it is hard to take. The one who did the shameful behavior apparently feels shameless. The one against whom the violation was made feels terrible shame.

Do you realize that God wraps His heart up in us? Do you realize that the passion, jealousy, and fierceness of love appropriate for guarding a marriage are just a whisper of the emotions God feels for us and our actions toward Him? We do shameful things, and Jesus bore the shame of it. It's a pretty amazing thought, but that's not the end of it. His response is to stay in the relationship. He disciplines us; He confronts and challenges us; He rebukes us and storms into our lives with passion; but above all, He never leaves us or forsakes us.

NOW IT'S YOUR TURN . . .

We encourage you to spend several days reading through Ezekiel 16. This allegory uses the shame of sexual sin to tell the story of Israel's unfaithfulness to God. Representing Himself as the betrayed husband, God let us know that He felt what a betrayed husband feels: shame, anger, and the torment of rejected love. His people were beloved, rescued orphans who turned from the rich tenderness of a husband to pursue an exponentially degrading promiscuity.

This chapter is graphic and uncomfortable. Some of you who read it will protest, "I really don't believe I'm that bad." But others will wonder, "How does God know how utterly ugly I am?"

Look carefully at how many times God made a statement similar to the one in verse 43—"You did not remember the days of your youth." Why is it important to remember what we were given and what we have squandered?

- How do you respond to the immensity of God's emotions in this chapter?
- How can He be holy and yet so jealous (see verse 38)?
- If His love is wise, sacrificial, perfectly pure, and always intent on blessing us, then what does it mean that He is also jealous for us?
- How do you respond to His jealous love?
- Look at the last sentence in Ezekiel 16. Who takes complete responsibility for our cleansing and restoration?

PAUSE TO RECEIVE:
DON'T WAIT

The words of an old hymn by Josh Hart may be the best way to end our conversation:

Come, ye sinners, poor and wretched,
Weak and wounded, sick and sore;
Jesus, ready, stands to save you,
Full of pity, joined with power.
He is able, He is able;
He is willing; doubt no more.

Come, ye needy, come, and welcome,
God's free bounty glorify;
True belief and true repentance,
Every grace that brings you nigh.
Without money, without money
Come to Jesus Christ and buy.

Let not conscience make you linger,
Nor of fitness fondly dream;
All the fitness He requireth
Is to feel your need of Him.
This He gives you, this He gives you,
'Tis the Spirit's rising beam.

Come, ye weary, heavy laden,
Bruised and broken by the fall;
If you tarry 'til you're better,
You will never come at all.
Not the righteous, not the righteous;
Sinners Jesus came to call.[4]

God's last invitation in His Word says the same thing: "The Spirit and the bride say, 'Come!' And let him who hears say, 'Come!' Whoever is thirsty, let him come; and whoever wishes, let him take the free gift of the water of life" (Revelation 22:17).

NOW IT'S YOUR TURN . . .

Will you come? The invitation of Christ is to come. He invites us into His presence again and again. Throughout the Gospels Christ invited people to follow Him. In Matthew 11:28-30 He urged us to come to Him when we are worn out with ourselves and with all that's put upon us. In John 7:37-38 He promised that if we come to Him because we are thirsty, He will overflow our hearts with the real life that only the Spirit can give. Coming to Christ is a journey, just as learning to walk toward our shame is a journey. We often think of "coming to Christ" as salvation—and it does mean that—but it also means returning to our lover, our husband we have betrayed. Coming to Christ through our shame is indeed long and dark, and we need His strength to do it. Will you pray for strength to make that journey?

Christ is not just a leader looking for followers. He is a brother seeking out His family; He is a lover seeking His bride. He's longing for connection, a meal together, a shared life with us. And He's promised never to leave us. That changes everything! The journey of following Christ and the journey of walking toward our shame is the same journey. He has promised to walk with us, guiding, strengthening, correcting, and healing because He wants to be with us. If you have not hit the trail with Him, you can today. He really is there, at the door, and He is hoping you will invite Him in.

Notes

Chapter 2: Poisoned Barbs and Deep Wounds
1. *The Matrix*, DVD, directed by Andy Wachowski and Larry Wachowski (Burbank, CA: Warner Bros. Pictures, 1999).

Chapter 3: True Roots and Faulty Tactics
1. Gilbert K. Chesterton, *Orthodoxy* (Nashville: Thomas Nelson, 2000), 176.

Chapter 4: Facing More Faulty Tactics
1. Graham Greene, *The End of the Affair* (New York: Penguin Group, 2004), 80–81.

Chapter 5: The Valley of Trouble or the Door of Hope?
1. The New Testament words about what it means to be in God's family are powerful. Take time to look at Romans 8:12-17 and Hebrews 2:10-18.

Chapter 6: A Journey over Time
1. A title of a well-known sermon by Jonathan Edwards, a New England minister, delivered in Enfield, Connecticut, on July 8, 1741.

Chapter 7: Beauty for Ashes: The Shame Exchange

1. C. S. Lewis, *The Great Divorce* (San Francisco: HarperSanFrancisco, 1973), 61–62.

Chapter 8: A Place for Me at the Table

1. John Calvin, *Institutes of the Christian Religion*, Book I: The Knowledge of God the Creator, trans. Henry Beveridge (Grand Rapids, MI: Eerdmans, 1970), 37.

2. Details about George Herbert's life are found in the introduction remarks to *The Oxford Authors: George Herbert and Henry Vaughan*, ed. Louis L. Martz (Oxford: Oxford University Press, 1990), xv–xxvi.

3. George Herbert, *The Temple: Sacred Poems and Private Ejaculations*, ed. N. Ferrar (Cambridge: T. Buck and R. Daniel, 1633), http://rpo.library.utoronto.ca/poem/979.html.

4. Joseph Hart, *Hymns Composed on Various Subjects*, 6th ed. (London: 1759), http://www.igracemusic.com/hymnbook/hymns/c08.html.

About the Authors

STEVE AND SALLY BREEDLOVE have spent their life together pastoring churches in the United States and Canada. They have been married for thirty-five years and live in Chapel Hill, North Carolina. They have five children, three of whom are married, and five grandchildren.

Steve received a ThM and DMin from Dallas Theological Seminary. He is the rector of All Saints Anglican, Chapel Hill–Durham. He has spoken in numerous countries, training pastors in leadership development. He is the leader for the Apostle's Mission Network of the Anglican Mission in America.

Sally is the author of *Choosing Rest* and a contributor to several other books. She speaks frequently at retreats and conferences. Together with Jennifer Ennis, she has started JourneyMates, a small-group spiritual-direction ministry.

RALPH AND JENNIFER ENNIS have served with The Navigators since 1975. Currently Ralph serves with The Navigators National Training Team. Some of his publications include *Breakthru: Discover Your Spiritual Gifts and Primary Roles; SuccessFit: Discovering Your Decision Making Preferences;* and *Searching the Ordinary for Meanings.* Ralph has a master's degree in intercultural relations.

Jennifer counsels in a private-practice office and serves on The Navigators National Counseling Team. Together with Ralph and others, she has written *An Introduction to the Russian*

Soul and *The Issue of Shame in Reaching People for Christ.* In 2006 she and Sally Breedlove began JourneyMates—a small-group spiritual-direction ministry for Christian leaders.

Ralph and Jennifer have been married for thirty-five years and live in Raleigh, North Carolina. They have four married children and ten grandchildren.

NavPress Resources for more tough issues.

Deceived by Shame, Desired by God

Cynthia Spell Humbert
978-1-57683-219-6

Shame often convinces us we are irreparably damaged at our very core. The Enemy wants you to believe this lie. But God says that there is nothing about you or your past that cannot be redeemed. Learn how the healing love of God can bring good out of your darkest, most shameful secrets. Includes discussion questions.

Inside a Cutter's Mind

Jerusha Clark with Dr. Earl Henslin
978-1-60006-054-0

Best-selling author Jerusha Clark, with Dr. E. Henslin, tackles one of the most disturbing trends among teens today. Drawing from a rich source of research and interviews, Jerusha explores the complex problem of cutting. With an empathetic ear and a compassionate voice, she brings light to a very dark condition and delivers hope to victims and their loved ones.

The CONNECT Bible study series

Ralph Ennis, Dennis Stokes, Judy Gomoll, Rebecca Goldstone, Christine Weddle

The CONNECT Bible study series provides a foundational study format for lifelong character transformation. Deeply biblical and rooted in Scripture, each study is relevant to real-life issues. You'll notice a grace-based approach to faith, so no matter where you are in the journey, freedom and acceptance can be yours. Each study in the six-book series is ten weeks and can be done as a group or individually. Reflective journal also available for the CONNECT series: *Identity: Becoming Who God Says I Am.*

To order copies, call NavPress at 1-800-366-7788 or log on to
www.navpress.com.